"This is a great way to protec[...] [...]—especially parents—should re[...] [...] this book."

"In this fantastic book, Rick Stedman shares personally and powerfully how we can grow in our faith through praying the armor of God. Prayer is one of the most life-giving and mysterious practices in which we can engage, and Rick models for us how to pray for those we love. *Praying the Armor of God* teaches us a lot about the heart of God and the joy of taking our cares and concerns to him. This is a book to read, apply, and share with others."

"If you've ever asked how parents can help their teenagers develop a strong faith in today's crazy world, one of the answers is in this book. *Praying the Armor of God* is a creative, easy to remember, and effective way for parents to stay spiritually engaged in their child's life. Read it...and practice it daily!"

"Good parents have always wanted to protect their children from physical dangers, but what are we doing to protect our children spiritually? In his new book, Rick Stedman provides the extra help and practical advice that busy parents need. In addition, his approach can help protect spouses, friends, and even prodigals from threats against their hearts and souls. Individuals, families, and even our world would be better if everyone were to daily follow his advice."

"This book not only equips you with a powerful prayer method, it's saturated with insights into the Word of God. We all want to intercede and pray more, and this gives us an easy way to shield those we love. Like young David readying himself to fight Goliath, Rick is clear that no human armor nor self-prepared armor will do. We need the armor that only God can provide as we fight the giants of the spiritual world."

—Lance Hahn, senior pastor,
Bridgeway Christian Church, Rocklin, California

"Every Christian parent I know, including me, wants the same thing. We want to see God at work in the lives of our kids. Rick's new book provides practical help in using the one tool God has given to impact the people we love—prayer. I have used the plan in this book with my kids and my friends. I recommend this to parents, couples, singles, and especially pastors. Buy it, read it, and most of all, put it into practice."

—Ray Johnston, senior pastor, Bayside Church,
Granite Bay, California, author of *The Hope Quotient*

"Christ's sufficient provision of spiritual armor is available to every believer. This book makes it readily applicable to your heart and your home, seven days a week."

—Daniel Henderson, president, Strategic Renewal

"It's finally here—a book about the armor of God and how to protect those you love. Let this true warrior, Pastor Rick Stedman, help you become a warrior in God's kingdom with a common sense way to arm yourself for spiritual warfare. This is a book for anyone who wants to protect their families, their country, and their faith."

—Lt. Gen. (Ret.) William Boykin, executive vice president,
Family Research Council

"Praying on the armor of God has never been so practical. Rick Stedman provides for us a simple way to bring God's protective power into the lives of the people we love."

—Dave Butts, chairman, America's National Prayer Committee

# PRAYING THE ARMOR OF GOD

## RICK STEDMAN

HARVEST HOUSE PUBLISHERS
EUGENE, OREGON

*Cover by Garborg Design Works, Savage, Minnesota*

*Backcover author photo by Jodi Burgess*

Published in association with the Books & Such Management, 52 Mission Circle, Suite 122, PMB 170, Santa Rosa, CA 95409-5370, www.booksandsuch.com.

**PRAYING THE ARMOR OF GOD**
Copyright © 2015 Rick Stedman
Published by Harvest House Publishers
Eugene, Oregon 97408
www.harvesthousepublishers.com

Library of Congress Cataloging-in-Publication Data
   Stedman, Rick.
   Praying the armor of God / Rick Stedman.
      pages cm
   ISBN 978-0-7369-6069-4 (pbk.)
   ISBN 978-0-7369-6070-0 (eBook)
   1. Spiritual warfare. 2. Prayer—Christianity. I. Title.
   BV4509.5.S74 2015
   248.3'2—dc23

                                       2014021862

**Printed in the United States of America**

20 21 22 23 / VP-JH / 10 9 8 7 6 5

# CONTENTS

To our three children,
Micah, Noah, and Jesse,
with the prayer that God would
put on each of you his full armor to
protect you and strengthen you,
"so that when the day of evil comes,
you may be able to stand your ground,
and after you have done everything, to stand."
(Ephesians 6:13)

# Introduction

**D**o you desire to improve your prayer life? I certainly do. In fact, I've been on a quest to improve my prayer life for years. I've read books, attended seminars, filled journals, listened to countless sermons, and preached over a hundred sermons on prayer. One year I taught fifty-two weeks in a row on prayer, which we called: "2001, A Prayer Odyssey." In three decades of ministry, it was the only sermon series that people requested I repeat the following year. I even chose to focus my doctorate of ministry on prayer, primarily in order to deepen my devotional life.

But the most meaningful, practical, and easy-to-remember method of prayer for me has been praying the armor of God.

In this book, I share my journey with you. Part 1 explains *why* we should pray the armor of God, including what the different pieces of the armor signify. Part 2 is a guidebook for daily prayer, illustrating *how* we can pray the armor of God.

How is this book different from other books on prayer? It's this: the pieces of the armor of God are arranged to correspond to the seven days of the week. Since you already know the days of the week, you can easily remember how to pray the armor of God. For instance: **S**undays we **S**trap on the Belt of Truth, **T**uesdays we **T**read in the Shoes of Peace, **F**ridays we **F**ight with the Sword of the Spirit, and so on.

In the beginning, you may want to pray the Part 2 prayers verbatim. Just pick a day of the week or a weekly topic, and pray one of the suggested prayers for those you love. If you pray one page per day, corresponding to each day of the week, you will finish in about ten weeks. Then you can start over and do it again…and again.

After a while, you will naturally memorize the essential elements, and the prayers will take on your own voice. You may be driving in a car, taking a walk, or lying in bed and feel drawn to prayer. You will think: *Well, today is Sunday, so I'll strap the belt of truth on those I love.* You begin to ask God to reveal his truth in your life, to fill your spouse with his truth, and for your kids to love truth and desire to be people of honesty. You may pray for your friends to be led by truth, your church to be a beacon of truth, your nation to return to truth, and the whole world to discover God's truth. It's a great way to pray! Plus,

- Parents and grandparents can help their kids—even prodigals—through prayer.
- Spouses can pray for one another and for growth in their marriage in key areas.
- Singles can pray for friends—or for their future spouses and families.
- Women can pray these essential qualities into the lives of those they love.
- Men may finally find, in this method, an enjoyable way to pray. Armor, after all, is something most men can relate to. It's masculine. It's military. It's tough. Whereas men sometimes feel pressured in churches to act in touchy-feely ways, this allows men to draw close to God in a way that doesn't compromise manhood.

As we begin, here is my prayer for you:

*I pray, almighty Father, that as we pray the armor of God, you would clothe us with Jesus Christ himself, transform us into his image, comfort us by your Spirit, and protect us from the evil one. I pray that the readers of this book would be filled with your truth, cleansed by your righteousness, calmed by your peace, fortified by your faith, eternally protected by your salvation, instructed by your Word, and empowered to rest in prayer. In Jesus' name, amen.*

# PART ONE

How to Pray the Armor of God

# Why Pray the Armor of God?

*"If we follow Jesus and look only to His righteousness,*
*we are in His hands and under the protection of*
*Him and His Father. And if we are in communion*
*with the Father, nought can harm us."*

—Dietrich Bonhoeffer[1]

A few years ago I was driving my fourteen-year-old son home from school. Like every other parent on the planet, I asked, "How was school today?"

He casually replied, "School was okay—except my TA in English was stoned."

A surge of angry thoughts raced through my mind. First, I was mad at myself. I felt like a failure as a parent for allowing my son to attend a drug-infested high school. Plus, I was upset with our public education system. My child was exposed to someone—the teacher's assistant, no less—who was smoking pot. Should we yank him out of school? Should I talk to the teacher? The principal? The governor? The president? (Okay, I admit that my emotions were getting carried away a bit.)

Instead, I asked, "Is this the first time that's happened?"

"No, he's a real stoner, and he smokes pot every day."

This made me even more upset. My kid had been exposed to this before, and I was totally clueless. I asked, "Do other kids do drugs?"

"Of course."

"How about you?" I said, trying to seem calm. "Have you ever tried drugs or wanted to try them?"

"No way. Doing drugs is dumb. Those kids are idiots."

At that moment, I was both elated and scared. I was elated my son was standing strong against temptations and that he and I were having this conversation. During the rest of the drive home, we talked about drugs, temptation, and peer pressure. So on the one hand, it was a fantastic day for me as a dad.

But on the other hand, I was scared. How could I, as a father, protect my son in a public school environment? I couldn't be physically present with him. I couldn't get rid of all temptations. So what could I do? What would help my kids be safe in a world of moral and spiritual danger?

I'm sure that most parents share this concern. How can we protect our children against the onslaught of "a warped and crooked generation" (Philippians 2:15)? How can we defend ourselves and those we love against the "flaming arrows" of the enemy (Ephesians 6:16)?

These questions don't apply only to parents. How can married couples protect themselves from the temptations that bombard them? How can grandparents, neighbors, singles, or classmates protect their families and friends from the enemy who seeks to "kill and destroy" (John 10:10)? After all, our human defenses are no match for this enemy. Fortunately, the apostle Paul answers this question in Ephesians 6:11: "Put on the full armor of God, so that you can take your stand against the devil's schemes."

But just *how* does one put on the full armor of God? Paul says to do it but doesn't mention how. As a young Christian, I assumed this was something I had to do. So, for many years I tried to put this armor on myself. I tried to be truthful, peaceful, righteous, and so on. I'm sure you can guess the result. In spite of my sincere efforts, I failed repeatedly.

Then it hit me that since this is the armor of God, it probably was not something I could put on myself. I would need God to put it on and in me. So, rather than *trying* to be peaceful, I asked God to *clothe* and *fill* me with his peace.

In other words, I began to *pray* the armor of God.

## How to Put on the Armor

Paul ends the armor of God section of his letter to the Ephesians with this: "And pray in the Spirit on all occasions with all kinds of prayers and requests. With this in mind, be alert and always keep on praying for all the Lord's people" (6:18). In other words, he essentially says, "Keep praying about it."

This was a thrilling insight for me, and I began to pray the armor of God with gusto. At first, I prayed through the whole armor of God every day for myself, for my family members (one at a time), for my friends, for my church, and for the world. But this was overwhelming, and the topics were too important to cover quickly. So I focused on one piece of armor per day. I found this to be more manageable and enjoyable.

But there was a problem: I would sometimes forget which piece of armor I prayed for on the previous day, so I would start the list again from the beginning. Over time, I saw that I was praying more often for the belt of truth than the helmet of salvation or the sword of the Spirit. Then one day I noticed there were six pieces to the armor of God, plus the instruction to "pray in the Spirit on all occasions" (6:18). I realized that these seven topics would pair nicely with the seven days of the week, and I developed a simple memory device to help me (and our church members) remember which piece of armor to pray each day. Since you have already memorized the days of the week, you can easily memorize and utilize the armor of God in prayer.

> **S**unday: **S**trap on the Belt of Truth
> **M**onday: **M**ake Fast the Breastplate of Righteousness
> **T**uesday: **T**read in the Shoes of Peace
> **W**ednesday: **W**ield the Shield of Faith
> **Th**ursday: **Th**ink Within the Helmet of Salvation
> **F**riday: **F**ight with the Sword of the Spirit
> **S**aturday: **S**teadfastly Pray in the Spirit

I can be driving, sitting at my desk, or out walking and feel the need to pray. My first thought is, *Okay, what day of the week is it? Well, it's Wednesday, so I need to wield the shield of faith.* I pray for God to increase my faith, I pray for God to fill my wife with faith, and I pray for my kids to always be people of faith. I pray for my friends to be strengthened in their faith, for our church to be a place where we fight, side by side, the good fight of faith. I pray for our nation to return to the faith it was founded upon, and I pray for people throughout the world to have the eyes of their hearts enlightened to the saving faith found in Jesus.

Or if it's Thursday, I pray, *God, please help me think within the helmet of salvation.* I continue on this course every day of the week and thereby pray the armor of God in a systematic and enjoyable way.

If you'd like to learn to pray the armor of God, I encourage you to begin right now. Don't read the whole book before you pray. Instead, pray as you go. Make this a prayer journey. As you read, take time to pause and pray from time to time, especially over the Scriptures. So let's begin: take a moment, focus your thoughts, and pray this prayer aloud now:

Lord,

> I want to put on your full armor through prayer, and I want
> my loved ones to be protected from evil.
> Teach me, through your Word, how to pray on the armor of
> God for myself and for those I love.
> In Jesus' name, amen.

## Living in a Battle Zone

Before we learn to pray each piece of armor, we might first ask, "Why do we need armor, anyway?" The answer is: we are in the midst of a dangerous spiritual battlefield, with demonic arrows flying at us. Without the right armor, we surely will be wounded.

Christians often forget this. A woman in our church once called me, quite distraught. She and her husband were committed Christians and had raised their children to love the Lord and be involved in church. She was shocked and mortified to discover that her teenage daughter was experimenting with sex. "How could this happen?" she exclaimed. "She knows we think this is terribly wrong."

A part of my response to her was, "You have an enemy who is trying to destroy your family. If he can attack one of your kids, he will. You and your family are in a battle zone, and a fiery dart from the enemy has hit your daughter."

"But I thought Christians were protected from Satan's attacks!" she said. "I never thought this could happen to us. What do I do now?"

Every pastor has received calls like this. The evidence is compelling: We are living on the battlefield. Spiritual warfare is very real. We have an enemy that is out to destroy us. "Your enemy the devil prowls around like a roaring lion looking for someone to devour" (1 Peter 5:8). According to the Bible, this war has been going on since the creation of the world.

In Ephesians 6:10-12, the apostle Paul describes the reality of this daily conflict:

> Finally, be strong in the Lord and in his mighty power. Put on the full armor of God, so that you can take your stand against the devil's schemes. For our struggle is not against flesh and blood, but against the rulers, against the authorities, against the powers of this dark world and against the spiritual forces of evil in the heavenly realms.

On a philosophical level, this helps answer some of life's hardest questions. Have you ever wondered why life is so difficult? Why bad things happen to good people, or why life seems to be such a series of struggles? Why committed Christians have a hard time staying married and why churches go through acrimonious splits? Why, in spite of all our cultural and technological advances, we still can't achieve world peace? The reality of spiritual warfare provides an answer: life is difficult because we have an incredibly malicious, highly organized, persistent, and darkly devious enemy who is out to destroy us.

Let me say this bluntly: every day, your evil foe sets his sights to destroy your marriage, your kids, your friends, your church…everyone and everything you care about. What are you doing to protect them? Try beginning with this prayer,

Lord,
I want my loved ones to be protected with the full armor of God.
But Lord, we have enemies who don't want this to happen.
They want us to remain vulnerable and unprotected.

Now that I realize this, I pray even more urgently and fer-
vently, please put your armor on those I love.
In Jesus' name, amen.

## Fasten Your Seat Belts

How can we protect those we love from the evil one and his nefari-
ous forces? The answer is just common sense: we need to put on spiritual
armor when we start our days, much like we fasten our seat belts when
we get into our cars. Just as we can strap our kids into their car seats physically, we can pray the armor of God on them spiritually.

When I was a kid, cars didn't have seat belts, we didn't use sunscreen,
and no one wore bike helmets. Our parents taught us to look both ways
before playing in the street. Parents today are so maniacal about safety that
kids aren't even allowed in the street. Today's kids have seat belts fastened,
bicycle helmets on, and antiseptic hand gel in lunch bags. (The emphasis on safety sometimes is funny. One father took his family on a vacation
drive, and happened to pass a nudist colony. As he sped past, his young
son noticed some cyclists and said, "Dad—did you notice? They weren't
wearing…any helmets!")

Safety preparedness is a good thing, and parents are wise to protect
their kids physically. My plea is for parents to do the same thing spiritually. Unfortunately, many seem to be unaware they are in the middle of a
spiritual war zone. They don't realize that as their kids go off to school, the
evil one has his sights on them and has a plan that very day to harm them.
They need protection. Spiritually, life is no picnic—it's a battle.

Once we grasp this, the sensible question is: how can we protect ourselves and our loved ones against this enemy? Fortunately, after Paul
explains the reality of our battle with evil, he tells us what to do:

> Therefore put on the full armor of God, so that when the
> day of evil comes, you may be able to stand your ground,
> and after you have done everything, to stand. Stand firm
> then, with the belt of truth buckled around your waist,
> with the breastplate of righteousness in place, and with

your feet fitted with the readiness that comes from the gospel of peace. In addition to all this, take up the shield of faith, with which you can extinguish all the flaming arrows of the evil one. Take the helmet of salvation and the sword of the Spirit, which is the Word of God.

And pray in the Spirit on all occasions with all kinds of prayers and requests. With this in mind, be alert and always keep on praying for all the Lord's people (Ephesians 6:13-18).

Before we move ahead, let's pause again for a moment of prayer. Pray the following prayer aloud to your loving Lord.

Lord,
This is beginning to make sense to me. I understand the need to fasten seat belts, and I'm very careful to protect my family physically.
Now I realize my family also needs protection spiritually, so teach me how to be diligent to pray your armor on those I love.
In Jesus' name, amen.

## Are We Strong Enough to Fight This Enemy?

Paul repeats himself in Ephesians 6:10-13, saying twice: "Put on the full armor *of God*." His repetition is intentional: it drives home the fact that we are not strong enough to fight against this vicious foe alone. If we try to fight with our own strength and protect ourselves with human armor, we will fail miserably. But that's exactly what most of us are doing. This is why Paul emphasizes that we must fight in the strength and power of the Lord, and we must be equipped with his armaments and not merely our own.

Indeed, confession is good for the soul, so let's confess to the Lord our need to rely on him and not our own strength:

Lord,

> I am not strong enough to fight the evil one. If I try to fight
>     him with my own strength, I will fail miserably.
> In Jesus' name, amen.

Pray it again…and then a third time!

This is why it is so crucial that we learn to *pray* the armor of God. To be honest, it has taken me many years—and repeated failure—to learn this. In the past I was taught to logically analyze each piece of armor. Then, I was encouraged to *try really hard to be those things.*

For instance, I was taught the biblical understanding of truth, and I was then directed to *try* to live that way. The image of the belt of truth as the armor *of God* melted away, and I was instructed to *try* to speak truthfully, to *try* to act truthfully, and to *try* to live truthfully. I was supposed to *try* to hang out with truthful friends, and *try* to challenge dishonest people to realize the error of their ways. In short, I was unwittingly *trying to create a piece of armor for myself.* It was my job to be truthful, which is to say that the armor would be as strong as I was able to make it.

But that was precisely the problem. I'm not strong enough to make my own armor, and neither are you. None of us can fight successfully on our own power. Remember, Paul said we are to "be strong in the Lord and in his mighty power." Truthfully, I can't trust myself to be completely truthful—even with myself. So a belt of my own design and making isn't going to be sufficient. I don't need my belt of truth around me; I need *the Lord's* belt of truth. It's an admirable and important goal to try to be truthful, but God's belt is infinitely stronger.

Let's try that prayer of confession again, with an added request:

Lord,

> I am not strong enough to fight the evil one. If I try to fight
>     him with my own strength, I will fail miserably.
> And if I try to arm myself against him, I will also fail
>     completely.
> Give me the wisdom to rely only on your armor, Lord.
> In Jesus' name, amen.

It's natural, at this point, to wonder whom we should pray for first: ourselves or our loved ones? Personally, I like the advice given by airlines. During the preflight safety speech, passengers are counseled that in the event of an emergency, they are to secure their own oxygen masks before they try to affix their children's. In the same way, it makes sense to pray the armor of God onto ourselves first, to get ourselves spiritually right before God. Then we are better able to pray for those we love.

This will be an important part of our prayer journey in this book. First, we can pray each prayer for ourselves, and then pray it for those we love, one at a time, by inserting their names. Let's give it a try. Pray again the same prayer, this time for someone who is dear to you:

Lord,

_____ is not strong enough to fight the evil one.
If _____ tries to fight him with his/her own strength, _____ will fail miserably.
And if _____ tries to arm himself/herself against him, _____ will also fail completely.
Give _____ the wisdom to rely only on your armor, Lord.
In Jesus' name, amen.

Now pray this again for someone else you love, and another, and another. In time, you will learn not only to adapt the prayers of this book for those you love, but you will also learn how to pray Scripture personally and powerfully.

## How Does the Armor of God Work?

As we learn to pray the armor of God, notice that Paul twice said to put on the *full* armor of God. Some Christians naively believe (maybe unconsciously) that they are protected from evil because they have been saved. "Oh, I'm saved, so I don't need anything else." They indeed may have on the helmet of salvation, but they still are vulnerable to attack. Other Christians may feel that because they are persons of peace (they have on the shoes of peace) they are protected. But they leave the rest of their body and soul open to attack. If we want to protect our loved ones and ourselves, we need to pray on the *full* armor of God because God's armor works best when all the pieces are in place, not just a few.

Before I learned how to pray the armor of God, I prayed diligently for those I love, but I emphasized some aspects of the Christian life over others. The sevenfold method of praying the armor of God solved this problem. Praying the armor of God has taught me to pray in a balanced, comprehensive way since I desire my loved ones to be fully armed.

Praying the armor of God also taught me to *not* focus on evil. I was shocked to discover that, in Ephesians 6:10-18, Paul's instructions on how to defend ourselves against evil have *very little to do with evil*. In my opinion, this is where some books on spiritual warfare go astray from the biblical text. They try to fight against evil by concentrating on the different schemes and ploys of the enemy. Instead, the biblical way to engage in warfare and fight the darkness is not to concentrate on the darkness. We fight the enemy by focusing on the Lord.

For instance, in Ephesians 6:10, Paul doesn't say to be strong in deliverance tactics, in exorcism prayers, or in our understanding of evil. Instead, he writes, "be strong in the Lord and in his mighty power." The way we defeat evil and darkness is by focusing on Jesus. After all, what is the armor of God except the very qualities of Jesus himself? He is Truth, Righteousness, Peace, the Word, and so on. As followers of Christ, we fight best by clothing ourselves with the very character and person of Christ, and then by allowing the light of Jesus to shine in and through us. In fact, to the Christians in Rome, Paul specifically connects these themes of armor, light, and being clothed with Christ: "So let us put aside the deeds of darkness and put on the armor of light…clothe yourselves with the Lord Jesus Christ" (Romans 13:12,14).

Of course, this is just common sense in the natural world. How do we get rid of the darkness when we go into a dark room late at night? Do we look at the darkness, study the darkness, and speak against the darkness? Do we yell in a loud voice, "Darkness, be gone!" or strongly say, "Darkness, I rebuke you"? Of course not. *We turn on the light.* It's the same in the supernatural realm. To get rid of the darkness of evil, we turn on the light of Christ. We bring Jesus into the situation, which is to ask him to fill us and, by his very presence, shine the light of glory. Light always conquers darkness. Light always prevails. Focus on Jesus rather than the evil one; it works better and it's safer for your soul.

With this in mind, let's take a moment to pause and pray. Let's combine the prayers we've learned so far into a complete, heartfelt prayer to God, and let's finish by praying a few words from Ephesians 6:10:

Lord,

> I'm not strong enough to fight the evil one. If I try to fight him with my own strength, I will fail completely.
> And if I try to arm myself against him, I will fail miserably.
> Instead, I ask you to strengthen me, Lord, with your mighty power.
> I understand the need for physical protection; now I realize my need for spiritual protection.
> I ask you to put on me the very character of Christ, because it's light that overcomes the darkness.
> I ask you to put on me your full armor, O God, so I can take my stand against the devil's schemes.
> In Jesus' name, amen.

I suggest that you use this simple prayer, or something like it, to begin your daily time of "praying the armor of God." I like to pray some form of this introductory prayer for myself before I pray on the specific piece of armor for that day. Next, I usually pray some variation of this prayer for my wife, by name:

Lord,

> My wife, Amy, is also not strong enough to fight the evil one.
> If she tries to fight him with her own strength, she will fail completely.
> And if she tries to arm herself against him, she will fail miserably.
> Instead, I ask you to strengthen her, Lord, with your mighty power.
> As she understands the need for physical protection, help her grasp her need for spiritual protection.
> I ask you to put on her the very character of Christ because it's light that overcomes the darkness.

I ask you to put on her your full armor, O God, so that she
    can take her stand against the devil's schemes.
In Jesus' name, amen.

I suggest you give this a try right now. Pray the preceding prayer aloud, but substitute the name and pronouns of a person of significance in your life. For instance, begin the prayer with, "Lord, I pray for my boyfriend, Alex…" or "Lord, I pray for my neighbor, Karen…"

After this introductory prayer, I pray the specific armor of the day for my wife. Next, I pray the same for my three children, one by one. At this point the routine changes, and I may pray for my parents, my siblings, extended family, or close family friends. Or I may feel led to pray for a coworker, our church body, our community, our government, our nation, or even our world. If we just pray for a few people each day, in a few months, we can cover a lot of ground. Once you get the hang of it, the prayers flow smoothly and naturally. (The second half of this book will guide you through this process.) After praying the armor of God for myself and a few others, I finish my prayer time with other specific requests (such as prayers for those who are ill, in need, and so on). It's a great way to start the day.

## How to Protect Those You Love

On the day my son told me that a teacher's assistant at his high school was stoned, I knew that a great way to protect him was to keep the lines of conversation open, to continue talking and encouraging him. I also knew that I needed to monitor his friendships and keep an eye out for any slippage. But as I drove home, I found myself praying silently for him, even as we continued to talk and drive. I prayed a silent prayer of thanks—and then several intense prayers of protection:

Lord,

Please protect my son from evil forces.
Please continue to keep his heart turned toward you.
Please help him withstand the many temptations at his high
    school, and keep him pure and clear and sober-minded.

Give him wisdom beyond his years and help him be a light
    to these kids who need you and your love so desperately.
In Jesus' name, amen.

Then, naturally and easily, I prayed the armor of God upon him.

After years of praying in this manner, I can testify that it doesn't get boring or old. Now that my kids are grown and gone, I still enjoy walking through their rooms (often as I am brushing my teeth in the morning and evening) and praying the armor of God for them. When I'm done praying, I feel great. I can't really explain it, but I know:

- I've spent quality time with the Lord.
- I've prayed in a biblical, effective, and simple manner.
- I've been armed and empowered to face that day's battles.
- I've asked God to arm and protect those I love from spiritual warfare.
- I'm ready to look to God, this very day, to answer these prayers.

## Here's the Plan as We Proceed

In the remainder of Part 1, we will look at the seven pieces of the armor of God and how each fits with its day of the week. Before we begin praying the armor of God daily, it's helpful to understand how each piece of armor protected an ancient warrior, and how each corresponds to the character qualities of Christ. Why did Paul liken truth to a belt and peace to shoes? In addition, how might these relate to the different days of the week?

In Part 2, the daily prayer process will begin. We will pray every day for ten weeks, each day writing down the date and the person(s) prayed for. We will learn that each week has a different topic, which will give our prayer experience breadth. And most importantly, we will discover that all the prayers are full of Scripture, which will give us depth.

With that in mind, let's begin by learning why it is appropriate, on Sundays, to ask God to "strap on us the belt of truth."

# SUNDAY

## Strap on the Belt of Truth

The first piece of armor God directs us to put on is the belt of truth: "Stand firm then, with the belt of truth buckled around your waist" (Ephesians 6:14).

### Why a Belt?

We probably wouldn't have guessed that the very first item to guard us is a simple belt. After all, we're already on the battlefield and spiritual darts are being shot at us—now. Perhaps we would pick up a shield first, or put a breastplate over our hearts or a helmet to cover our heads. How could a skinny piece of rope or leather protect us?

Historically, for both Greek and Roman soldiers, their full armor was called *panoply* (which literally meant "a full suit of armor"). Wilbur Fields provides a good summary of the *panoply* in his commentary on the book of Ephesians:

> The historian Polybius (about 200 B.C.) wrote a description of Roman armor in his time. Polybius said that the Roman panoply consisted, in the first place, of a shield *(thureos)*, and that along with the shield was a sword *(machaira)*. Then next came two javelins *(hussoi)*, a helmet *(perikephalaia)* and a greave *(knemis)*. The majority, when they had further put on a bronze plate, measuring a span

every way, which they wore on their breasts, and called a heart guard *(kardiophulax)*, were completely armed. But those citizens who were assessed at more than 10,000 drachmae wore instead, together with the other arms, *cuirasses* made of chain mail. [2]

Paul's first item, the belt, was not even mentioned in Polybius's list of armor. Technically, a belt was not a piece of armor, but simply an essential piece of clothing for both soldiers and everyday citizens. It was not like the belts worn by police officers today, full of devices and holders for various weapons. It was not like, in comic book fashion, the famous "bat belt" from which Batman always had at his fingertips any crime-stopping or life-saving device needed. The belt of truth Paul is talking about isn't a military belt, an ammo holster, or a superhero belt.

Instead, Paul is referring to the simple strap—for the poor, probably just a piece of rope—that nearly all adults wore. In biblical times, most people wore simple tunics. A tunic was a single, rectangular piece of cloth, folded and sometimes roughly sewn on two sides, with holes cut for one's head and arms. Tunics would fall naturally along one's torso and down to the lower legs or ankles. Because tunics were not fitted, they would be cumbersome to walk or work in, and especially difficult to fight in. For this reason, a belt was strapped around one's waist to keep the flowing garment out of the way.

If a person were to run or fight, the lower portion of the tunic would be raised up and tucked under the belt, a process called "girding the loins." In fact, the word *gird* means "to encircle or bind something with a flexible band." This is just what the belt did for the tunic. It encircled and bound the loose and flowing parts of the tunic to the soldier's body so he could fight less encumbered, and it did the same for the civilian so he or she could work.

The image of utilizing a belt is found throughout the Bible. God instructed Moses how to eat the Passover meal when leaving Egypt: "This is how you are to eat it: with your cloak tucked into your belt, your sandals on your feet and your staff in your hand. Eat it in haste; it is the Lord's Passover" (Exodus 12:11). They were to eat in readiness to flee, symbolized by, as the older translations translated it, their "girded loins." In the same way, we believers are instructed by Jesus to be ready for his return by being "dressed ready for service" (Luke 12:35), which reads in some versions, "let your loins be girded about." Peter also uses the same expression concerning the believer's mental readiness (1 Peter 1:13).

In all of these cases, the point of girding a belt around one's waist is to prepare and ready oneself. To have "the belt...buckled about your waist" (Ephesians 6:14) simply means: *get ready for action*. So, to pray on the belt of truth signifies we understand a struggle is just ahead of us, and we are preparing ourselves for the fight.

### Why Truth?

Truth is necessary because we humans are habitual liars. We even lie to ourselves. Why is this? Jesus said, to the leaders of his day,

> You belong to your father, the devil, and you want to carry out your father's desires. He was a murderer from the beginning, not holding to the truth, for there is no truth in him. When he lies, he speaks his native language, for he is a liar and the father of lies. Yet because I tell the truth, you do not believe me! (John 8:44-45).

According to Jesus, our enemy, the devil, is "a liar," "the father of lies," and "there is no truth in him." While studies reveal that two-thirds of spouses lie to each other, and while over 90 percent of Americans lie routinely,[3] Satan lies *100 percent* of the time. There is *no* truth in him.

This is why it's so important to put on the belt of truth. Satan attacks and attaches himself to us when we deceive. When we lie, we "give the devil a foothold" (Ephesians 4:27). For me, this has been a revolutionary insight. In the past I thought a white lie was just a little sin. I came to realize, as a result of praying the armor of God, that lying is no minor matter. There is no such thing as a white lie; a lie is a lie. A small foothold is still a foothold—in fact, a foothold is small by definition.

Fortunately, into our world of deep and deceptive darkness, Jesus came to shine the light. The bad news is that Satan lies 100 percent of the time;

the good news is that Jesus is 100 percent truthful. Jesus said, "I am the way, the truth, and the life" (John 14:6). When we put on the belt of truth, his light, love, and truthfulness shine in us.

So why is the first item of armor *the belt of truth*? Why aren't we told to put on the belt of peace or the belt of salvation? The answer is this: truth is God's view of reality, which enables us to correctly add the additional pieces of armor. Without truth, how can we be sure that the breastplate of righteousness is really God's concept of righteousness and not some mistaken version of righteousness foisted on us by our culture? Without truth, how can we be sure any piece of armor is truly God's version: His view of peace? His understanding of faith? His definition of salvation? Yes, before we can put on any other piece of armor, with full assurance, we first must solidly pray on God's truth. In this deceptive world, only then can each ensuing piece of armor be correct.

I love Sundays, partly because I love praying truth into the lives of those I love. I pray we would cherish honesty, be repelled by dishonesty, and be able to discern the truth of a matter. I pray that Jesus himself, the Truth, would inhabit and reveal to us any self-deception and so fill us that there would be no room for darkness or satanic footholds.

Give it a try: pray aloud the following prayer, and start your week by prayerfully strapping on the belt of truth.

> Lord,
>
> > It's Sunday, so it's a great opportunity to strap on the belt of truth.
> > I pray for you to increase my understanding of your truth.
> > Please fill my wife/husband (if single, insert the name of a close friend) with truth in her/his inner being.
> > I pray for my kids (relatives) to always be people of honesty.
> > I pray for my friends to be strengthened in the truth.
> > I pray for our church to be a beacon of truth, for in this world, side by side, we fight the good fight of truth.
> > I pray for our nation to return to your truths, upon which it was founded, and
> > I pray for people throughout the world to have the eyes of

their heart enlightened to the saving truth found only in Jesus.

I pray this in his name who is Faithful and True. Amen.

Proverbs 23:23; Psalm 51:6; Proverbs 12:17; Psalm 119:28;  Matthew 5:14-15; Colossians 2:1; Ephesians 1:18; Acts 4:12; Revelation 19:11.

# MONDAY

## Make Fast the Breastplate
## of Righteousness

onday, Monday," sung by the Mamas and the Papas in 1966, became an enduring hit because it expressed exactly how most people feel on Mondays: it's a lousy day. It's the day we end our weekend of fun and go to our jobs singing the I-have-to-go-back-to-work blues. Many folks hate Monday; for them it's the worst day of the week. Maybe this is the reason more than a third of all sick days are taken on Mondays. We feel disheartened, which could be why the Mamas and the Papas said they felt like crying on Mondays. Can't trust that day.

But I love Mondays! When we pray the armor of God daily, each Monday is a terrific opportunity to protect those we love. And what does the apostle Paul suggest that we protect first? The answer is—our *hearts*.

### Why a Breastplate?

Paul instructs us in Ephesians 6:14 to put on the second item of armor. "Stand firm, then…with the breastplate of righteousness in place."

Why does Paul mention this piece of armor next? A soldier's breastplate was a piece of hammered metal molded to roughly contour to his chest, or if we believe Hollywood, to represent the pecs and six-pack that lay hidden underneath. (I'm now middle-aged, and I sometimes tell my congregation that I still have a six-pack—it's just hidden in my cooler.)

Much like today's Kevlar and bulletproof vests, the purpose of a breast-plate was to protect the vital organs, especially the heart. This is exactly what we need spiritually. We need protection for our spiritual center, which is metaphorically rendered as the heart. And here is the interesting connection: the Bible connects the heart with righteousness, or rather, the lack thereof.

### Why Righteousness?

The Bible says "There is no one righteous, not even one" (Romans 3:10), and "The heart is deceitful above all things and beyond cure" (Jeremiah 17:9). Of course, our culture doesn't understand this since it lacks the belt of truth. Statements such as "People are basically good," "All children are pure," and "As innocent as a child" are common. But these common-sense notions are not correct, for we are all born with a natural inclination toward evil. In Genesis, God said to Noah after the flood, "Never again will I curse the ground because of humans, even though every inclination of the human heart is evil from childhood" (Genesis 8:21).

What a surprise this is to modern (and postmodern) people, who glibly assume they should always "follow their hearts." A friend and I were once talking about this, when he suddenly took off his watch and said, "Rick, look at the inscription on the inside." On the gold-plated underside of his watch, these words were inscribed:

*"To my husband on our wedding day.*
*Follow your heart."*

Then he said to me, "My wife gave this to me on our wedding day. And guess what? I followed her advice, and she is now—as a result—my ex-wife." He went on to say, "Written on the back of this watch is the worst piece of advice I was ever given in my whole life. After this, when I was tempted, I followed my heart, and I ended up doing things that led to the ruin of our marriage."

Dear friends, don't "follow your heart." Our hearts lie to us.

### Can We Overcome Our Deceitful Hearts?

In spite of Jeremiah's clear warning that our hearts are deceitful, as a new Christian I thought I could overcome my deceptive heart. I assumed it was my job to be righteous, that is, to put the breastplate of righteousness on myself. So I'd try to be pure, try to be holy, and try to go a day without sin. But I just couldn't do it. When I did seem to have a good day, I found myself feeling prideful about it, which ruined my righteousness for the day. I was a failure either way. I learned I couldn't become righteous on my own power. Putting the breastplate of righteousness on myself never worked for me, just as it didn't for King David, or the apostle Paul, or anyone else in the Bible except for Jesus.

Instead, the only way to become righteous is to ask the Righteous One, Jesus Christ, into our hearts to take residence as Lord and Savior. The Bible is very clear: we cannot become righteous on our own. The prophet Isaiah said "all our righteous acts are like filthy rags" (Isaiah 64:6). Paul wrote, "If righteousness could be gained through the law, Christ died for nothing!" (Galatians 2:21). He told the Philippian believers his desire was to "be found in him, not having a righteousness of my own that comes from the law, but that which is through faith in Christ—the righteousness that comes from God on the basis of faith" (Philippians 3:9). And Paul wrote to the believers in Corinth: "God made him who had no sin to be sin for us, so that in him we might become the righteousness of God" (2 Corinthians 5:21).

No one can put on the breastplate of righteousness but Jesus. In fact, he already has. Isaiah wrote,

> So justice is far from us,
>     and righteousness does not reach us…
> The LORD looked and was displeased
>     that there was no justice.
> He saw that there was no one,
>     he was appalled that there was no one to intervene;
> so his own arm worked salvation for him,
>     and his own righteousness sustained him.
> He put on righteousness as his breastplate,
>     and the helmet of salvation on his head.
>                         (Isaiah 59:9,15-17)

The armor of God is *his armor*, not ours, so only God can handle its pieces and dress us with it. Isaiah himself experienced this and said, switching metaphors slightly,

> I delight greatly in the LORD;
> my soul rejoices in my God.
> For he has clothed me with the garments of salvation
> and arrayed me in a robe of his righteousness.
> (Isaiah 61:10)

The book of Revelation reflects this metaphor. After the triumphant return of Christ, each Christian martyr "was given a white robe" signifying, of course, the complete and utter righteousness that can be received only as a gift of God, and never something that one can earn or deserve (Revelation 6:11).

## Monday, Monday, How I Love that Day!

On Mondays, we pray with King David, "Create in me a pure heart, O God" (Psalm 51:10), and we believe that God will keep the promise he made through the prophet Ezekiel, "I will give you a new heart and put a new spirit in you; I will remove from you your heart of stone and give you a heart of flesh" (Ezekiel 36:26). On Mondays, as we pray on the breastplate of righteousness, how good it is to know that we are helping to protect, through prayer, the hearts of those we love.

Let's pray this right now, aloud, to our righteous Savior:

Lord,

> I pray on this Monday that you make fast the breastplate of righteousness.
> I pray that you would firmly fasten it around my heart, so integrity and uprightness will protect me.
> I pray for (insert names of spouse and children, or close friends), that you put on them the breastplate of righteousness; write faithfulness and love on the tablets of their hearts.

I pray for (insert names of extended family members), that
   you put on them your breastplate of faith and love.
Please guide them today in the paths of righteousness, for
   that is the way of life, and along that path is immortality.
I pray this in the name of the King of Righteousness. Amen.

   Psalm 25:21; Isaiah 59:17; Proverbs 3:3; 1 Thessalonians 5:8;
   Proverbs 8:20; Proverbs 12:28.

# TUESDAY

## Tread in the Shoes of Peace

Very few people love Tuesdays. The one exception might be Mardi Gras, which is French for "Fat Tuesday," the day before Ash Wednesday. (That's a day on which believers really need to pray on the full armor of God. Maybe we should start a "Fast Tuesday" counter-holiday.) But during most weeks and for most adults, on Tuesday it's time to dig in, to put the axe to the grindstone, our hand to the plow. It's a day of labor.

Since most of us work on Tuesdays, it's a good day to consider our careers (and the careers of those we love). What is the secret to success? Are successful people smarter, more talented, or harder workers? Are they just lucky? Do successful people have higher IQs or diplomas from more prestigious colleges? Surprisingly, none of the above factors is the number one predictor of successful careers. The number one factor is one's *relational* ability.[4] Relational ability not only helps at work; it also greatly enhances the potential for success in one's marriage, parenting, friendships, and neighborhoods—virtually every important area of life.

Most of these crucial areas are under siege today. Couples divorce, friendships dissolve, and neighbors get upset. Conflict is rampant. Is there something we can do to protect our loved ones from these and other relational disasters? Mercifully, there is. God has provided a spiritual weapon that can help keep our marriages, families, friendships and churches together. We need to become skilled conflict-resolvers, effective relationship-menders. In short, peacemakers.

Which is exactly the third piece of armor the apostle Paul counsels Christians to have: "your feet fitted with the readiness that comes from the gospel of peace" (Ephesians 6:15). On Tuesdays, we ask God to put on us the shoes of *shalom*.

## Why Shoes?

Once a Roman soldier secured his tunic around his waist with a belt and made fast his breastplate to protect his heart and other vital organs, he would be wise to tie on his shoes. The longer one waits to do this task, the more difficult it becomes due to the bulk of the remaining armor.

Like the belt, shoes were not mentioned in Polybius's list of the soldier's panoply; they were everyday items of adult clothing. For a Greek or Roman soldier, shoes were especially important. The terrain in the Middle East was—and still is—very dry and full of sharp stones. Soft moccasins quickly tear on the jagged rocks and don't provide the support needed to march long distances. Ancient military footwear was sometimes called sandals, but don't picture something like today's flip-flops. Josephus, the Jewish historian, said that the Roman soldiers had footwear that was made of layers of heavy leather, fashioned together and stapled with nails. It was very strong footwear, what we might compare to industrial-quality hiking sandals. In addition, their stiff soles offered stability and traction. Whereas peasants could walk barefoot and merchants could wear thin-soled slippers, Roman soldiers knew they were not ready for battle until their feet were fitted with proper shoes.

Additionally, footwear needs to be secured to a soldier's feet before he goes onto a battlefield. Whether the enemy is using arrows or bullets, the battlefield is the wrong place to bend down and retie one's shoelaces. That's why Paul said, "feet fitted with the *readiness*."

Shoes are also important for most athletes. I remember in high school, just before we ran onto the field to begin a game, our football coach often would say, "Now, men, check your shoes and laces. Make sure they are tied well, because you don't want to risk losing a touchdown over a loose shoelace." No experienced athlete gets on the field, hears the starting whistle, and says, "Well, I need to put my shoes on now." In the same way, as Christians we ask God to put on us his shoes of peace before we enter the battlefield. We prayerfully decide to be peacemakers before a conflict arises, not after.

## Why Peace?

To put it bluntly, many of us—Christians included—aren't very good at this. We don't resolve conflict well, and we struggle to maintain long-term relationships. In every relationship, conflict sooner or later raises its ugly head. No matter what Neil Sedaka sang, breaking up is *easy* to do. It's staying together that's hard.

I'm sure the only one happy about all this conflict is Satan himself, who seems to be an expert at dividing people. He started right at the beginning, dividing Adam and Eve from God in the Garden. He divided Isaac from Ishmael, Jacob from Esau, and Joseph from his ten older brothers. He divided the Hebrew nation into northern Israel and southern Judah, and he separated the Israelites from the Promised Land when they were taken into captivity in Babylon. The evil one has been at this for millennia, perfecting his craft of creating conflict and division. He even divided the heavenly host! He is the expert divider, the master of disaster (to borrow a line from the *Rocky* movies).

That the devil is the great divider should come as no surprise. Even the Greek word for demon, *daimon,* comes from the root word that means "to divide or separate." Our enemy, the devil, uses his demonic forces to separate and divide, with surprising effectiveness. This is why merely trying harder to be persons of peace will never bring success. There is a spiritual war being waged around us, and there are spiritual beings who are working to divide and conquer. We are not adequate to fight this battle on our own, which is why we need to pray for God to place his armor on us. If we don't, some of our most precious relationships will be broken in the years ahead.

## The Gospel of Peace

The good news (the gospel) is that Jesus, the Prince of Peace (Isaiah 9:6), has come and has defeated evil on the cross. He has won for us the victory, and a result of his victory is that we can now be filled with his peace.

Jesus said, "Peace I leave with you; my peace I give you," and "I have told you these things, so that in me you may have peace. In this world you will have trouble. But take heart! I have overcome the world" (John 14:27; 16:33). Think for a moment about these claims: "My peace" and "in me you may have peace." They are either some of the most arrogant statements ever uttered or the most awesome truths. Who else could say that but God himself, having come to earth as our Savior and King? This is also why Paul wrote,

> Do not be anxious about anything, but in every situation, by prayer and petition, with thanksgiving, present your requests to God. And the peace of God, which transcends all understanding, will guard your hearts and your minds in Christ Jesus (Philippians 4:6-7).

"The peace of God" is God's own peace, coming down upon earth and within the soul of the believer, because Jesus is the Prince of Peace. Clothed with Christ, we experience more than just the absence of conflict: we experience healthy relationships. After all, the Bible's word for peace, *shalom*, means a state of wholeness, completeness, health, and prosperity.

Do you desire a life filled with good for those you love? That they become peacemakers who are very successful in their key relationships? If so, then you will enjoy Tuesdays, when we pray that God clothes our loved ones with his *shalom*.

This is why I look forward to Tuesdays: after praying, I feel a deep, profound sense of calm, wellness, and tranquility. Though battles and wars are being waged in the spiritual realms around us, I sense that God is in control, and his peace will prevail. It's as if my heart and my mind take a deep breath together, sit back in the easy chair of my soul, and relax. I don't need to solve the problems in the world; instead, I pray for myself and those I love to be armed with the shoes of peace. I experience what Paul instructed, letting the peace that passes all understanding guard my heart and my mind as I trust in Christ Jesus. Try it for yourself:

Lord,

> I pray on this Tuesday that you help me "tread in the shoes of peace."

I pray that your peace would be a firm foundation for my
    life, and that you fill me with all joy and peace as I trust
    in you.

I pray for (insert names of spouse and children, or close
    friends), that you inspire them to be peacemakers and
    conflict-resolvers in this world so infected by conflict, dis-
    cord, and division.

I pray for (insert names of extended family members), that
    you help them, as far as it is possible, to be at peace with
    all people.

Please keep us in your perfect peace, for we trust in you.

I pray this in the name of the Prince of Peace. Amen.

> 2 Timothy 2:19; Romans 15:13; James 3:18; 1 Corinthians 1:10;
> Romans 12:18; Isaiah 26:3; Isaiah 9:6.

# WEDNESDAY

## Wield the Shield of Faith

In previous centuries, Wednesday was considered a day of bad luck. This was expressed in a clever rhyme, which first appeared in print in 1838 in A.E. Bray's *Traditions of Devonshire*:

> Monday's child is fair of face,
> Tuesday's child is full of grace,
> Wednesday's child is full of woe,
> Thursday's child has far to go,
> Friday's child is loving and giving,
> Saturday's child still works for a living,
> But the child who is born on the Sabbath Day
> Is bonny and blithe and good and gay.

Times and the meanings of words have changed (as the last line reveals), but this poem suggests that Wednesday was once considered a bummer of a day. It still is.

This is why, in the 1970s macabre TV comedy *The Addams Family*, the young girl was named Wednesday. In fact, her full name was Wednesday Friday Addams, since Friday was also considered by occultists to be an evil day due to the crucifixion (*contra* Bray). Even a national TV show to help children in foster homes find permanent adoptive families is called, not surprisingly, *Wednesday's Child*.

Though Christians don't believe in bad luck, Wednesday is still a tough day. As the day begins, the workweek is not yet half over. The halfway point isn't reached until noon. That's why the slang term for Wednesday is "hump day."

However, for Christians who pray on the armor of God daily, Wednesday can be a wonderful day, a day of faith. The apostle Paul instructed believers, after they had clothed themselves with truth, righteousness, and peace, to "take up the shield of faith, with which you can extinguish all the flaming arrows of the evil one" (Ephesians 6:16).

## Why a Shield?

Paul likens faith to a shield, and claims it protects us from *all* the flaming darts of the evil one. How is this possible? A shield can certainly protect us from arrows launched toward us, if our shield is in front of us. But how can attacks from the side or rear be prevented? Surely Satan assaults believers from all angles. I would even guess the evil one prefers to attack from the rear, by cowardly stabbing people in the back.

These questions are solved when we learn that the Romans used two different kinds of shields: a small shield for hand-to-hand combat, and a tall, oblong shield too big for hand-to-hand combat but perfectly suited for soldiers fighting together in formation, as a unit.

It is this second type of shield that Paul specified in Ephesians 6:16. This shield, called a *thureos,* was approximately two-and-a-half feet wide and four feet tall[5] and made of wood and covered with leather. Before being taken into battle, it would be soaked in water, making the leather stronger and less brittle. Plus, the wet leather helped douse any flaming arrows. Significantly, the Greek word *thureos* was also the word for a common, everyday door. The soldier who carried this shield into battle was literally carrying something akin to a small door. Why would a soldier carry such a bulky implement?

The answer is inspirational. As the soldiers marched together in formation, they kept one another safe from enemy arrows by walking shield-to-shield-to-shield. In this way, a legion of soldiers could march up to a city wall or an enemy's front line and be impervious to the arrows shot at them by opposing archers. Even if the soldiers were surrounded during battle, they could enclose themselves within their shields by constructing a defensive barrier, like a turtle's shell, under which the soldiers could hide. In antiquity, such a military formation was called a phalanx, which the three hundred Spartans used with great, albeit temporary, success in the renowned Battle of Thermopylae.

## Lone Ranger Christians

Here's the point: the shield of faith was never meant to be used by solo Christians. The shield of faith is to be used in formation, alongside other Christians who have also taken up their shield, their *thureos* of faith. To do so takes coordination, cooperation, commitment, and, supremely, trust. Soldiers had to be certain their brothers-in-arms would not falter or fade back due to fear; their lives depended upon how well each one held up his *thureos*.

Obviously, we twenty-first-century Christians could learn from their example. Many today think they can be Lone Ranger Christians. They sincerely believe they don't need to belong to a church; they can just visit around, hop and shop, pop in or out, and participate when and where they desire. They can study the Bible on their own; they can pray on their own; they can even worship on their own. They genuinely think they don't need responsibilities or accountability. They are spectators, not warriors.

This leaves them massively undefended. Probably sooner rather than later, solo Christians will be attacked by evil forces, and will find flaming arrows coming at them from all sides. They are vulnerable and at risk. They will be deeply wounded.

Plus, solitary believers are not a threat to the enemy. Alone, they cannot advance upon a city wall, they cannot frighten and defeat the enemy, and they cannot wreak havoc like a unified force. Both spiritual warfare and evangelism suffer when Christians are not strongly tied to one another in authentic Christian community. We need each other; it's the only way the shield of faith works. As Plato is rumored to have said, "We are twice armed if we fight with faith."

So pray the armor of God on those you love! You know they will be tempted and attacked—every day—by the evil one in this dark and twisted world. Pray that God would put on them his shield of faith, and that he would help them understand spiritual shields are only effective when Christians operate in groups. Pray that they profoundly grasp that Christianity is a team event, and it is very wise to get involved in a church.

## Why Faith?

The writer of Hebrews says, "Without faith it is impossible to please God" (Hebrews 11:6), and the prophet Habakkuk said, "The righteous will live by faith" (Habakkuk 2:4; Romans 1:17). Or as Paul put it, "We live by faith, not by sight" (2 Corinthians 5:7).

What is faith? My definition of Christian faith is *to live trusting in the Lord Jesus rather than ourselves.* This is a declaration that God, as revealed in Jesus, is more dependable than we are, that his will is better for us than our own, and that his ways are more just (Isaiah 55:6–56:1). We choose to trust in God rather than in ourselves.

Solomon, called the wisest person who ever lived, understood this. He said,

> Trust in the LORD with all your heart
> 　and lean not on your own understanding;
> in all your ways submit to him,
> 　and he will make your paths straight.
> Do not be wise in your own eyes;
> 　fear the LORD and shun evil.
> This will bring health to your body
> 　and nourishment to your bones.
> 　　　　　　　　　　　　　　(Proverbs 3:5-8)

Solomon also said,

> Do you see a man wise in his own eyes?
> 　There is more hope for a fool than for him.
> 　　　　　　　　　　　　　　(Proverbs 26:12)

In a similar vein, the prophet Isaiah said,

> Woe to those who are wise in their own eyes
> 　and clever in their own sight…
> Therefore, as tongues of fire lick up straw
> 　and as dry grass sinks down in the flames,
> so their roots will decay
> 　and their flowers blow away like dust;

for they have rejected the law of the LORD Almighty
and spurned the word of the Holy One of Israel.
(Isaiah 5:21,24)

I love that phrase "Do not be wise in your own eyes." Is there any truth to which we are more blind in today's secular society than this?

I love praying this for those I care about. On Wednesdays, I pray for my wife, our marriage, and our kids. I pray for our relatives, our church, and our nation. I pray that God puts his shield of faith around us all. I pray that God would help us grow to understand the value of faith. I pray we come to deeply believe one of the smartest things we can do is to have faith in God, and to live every moment of our lives in light of that faith. I pray God would help us to grow in the assurance of faith and confidence in the Bible. I pray the church might become stronger than ever before, filled with committed members who will love, serve, and protect each other as a team, through the ups and downs of life, until the Lord himself calls us home to glory. Finally, I even pray that atheists, agnostics, philosophers, educators, and scientists would all grasp that faith is an essential element in the human rational process, and by recognizing this process, they would open themselves to the validity of faith in God. What a great way to pray!

Lord,

> It's Wednesday, so I ask you to help us "wield the shield of faith."
> As the apostles asked Jesus, we pray, "Increase our faith."
> As the distraught father confessed, we each pray, "I do believe; help me overcome my unbelief."
> I pray that my spouse (or friend) could walk by faith, not sight.
> I pray for my kids (relatives) to always be people of faith.
> I pray for my friends to be strengthened in their faith, and for our church to fight, side by side, the good fight of faith.
> I pray for our nation to return to the faith upon which it was founded.

I pray for people throughout the world to find saving faith
in Jesus.

I pray this in his Faithful and True name. Amen.

> Luke 17:5; Mark 9:24; 2 Corinthians 5:7; 3 John 4; Colos-
> sians 2:7; 1 Timothy 6:12; Jeremiah 3:12; 2 Chronicles 7:14;
> Romans 1:8.

# THURSDAY

# Think Within the Helmet of Salvation

An idle brain is the devil's workshop." This well-known proverb is not from the Bible, but instead can be traced back to William Perkins, an English Puritan minister in the late 1500s. He wrote, in the quaint and pre-standardized spelling of his day, "The idle bodie and the idle braine is the shoppe of the deuill."[6]

Today, "the devil's workshop" has entered popular culture and is used as the title for novels, movies, a dangerous neighborhood in Batman's Gotham City, a sound studio in Minnesota, a jewelry store in Canada, an online knife-makers club, and a tobacco shop in California. "The devil's workshop," for some, now seems to be cool.

But what if this is *true*? If there is such a being as the devil (Christians believe this is the case since Jesus certainly did), is the mind a place where the devil might make his workplace, his home? Might the human brain be where the real wrestling match, the tug-of-war between good and evil, takes place? If so, not cool.

Yes, there is a battle going on in the minds of human beings. Paul said, "The god of this age has blinded the minds of unbelievers, so that they cannot see the light of the gospel that displays the glory of Christ, who is the image of God" (2 Corinthians 4:4). If we desire to win the battle for the minds of those we love, we must somehow find a way to protect the way we think. How can we protect our thought-life in this world of mental danger? The answer is the fifth piece of the armor of God: the "helmet of salvation" (Ephesians 6:17).

## Why a Helmet?

Roman military helmets were an essential part of the panoply. They usually were fashioned out of bronze, which was malleable and relatively easy to mold to fit one's head. Wealthier soldiers had helmets forged out of iron, a much more difficult process but also more durable and hard to penetrate. Poorer soldiers often wore helmets made of inexpensive leather, or several layers of leather for extra strength. A soldier could even fashion a leather helmet for himself and thus avoid the expense of a blacksmith. There was no excuse to go into battle with one's head unprotected.

Early helmets consisted of a simple shell or bowl, comparable to the shape of a modern baseball cap minus the bill, that covered one's cranium. A "shelf" was attached to the back of the basic helmet to protect the soldier's neck and shoulders. This shelf was made out of metal or leather and was securely fastened to the back of the helmet.

The Roman helmet also had cheek-pieces to protect the sides of one's face. The Greeks had decreased visibility and mobility due to the rigidity of their helmets, but the Romans solved this problem. They fastened metal or leather plates with hinges above each cheekbone to provide protection and also better movement than stationary cheek-pieces. These coverings were connected at the bottom with a leather strap—a chinstrap, if you will. This strap held the cheek-pieces in place and also cinched down the whole helmet so it remained securely on the soldier's head during battle.

During the first century, Roman soldiers sometimes added a small bill to the front of the helmet, probably to protect their eyes from the sun. If they could afford it, they also added ear coverings made of bronze.

## Why Salvation?

Spiritually, a helmet serves two main purposes: it protects our very survival, and it protects our minds. Let's deal with survival first. Obviously, without one's head, survival is impossible. This is why, I believe, Paul called the spiritual helmet in the armor of God the "helmet of salvation." Without salvation, one will not survive spiritually—especially beyond the grave.

Salvation is possibly the most important topic in the Bible. As Peter schooled the religious leaders of his day, "Salvation is found in no one else, for there is no other name under heaven given to mankind by which we must be saved" (Acts 4:12). Paul told the Ephesians, "You were dead in your transgressions and sins…But because of his great love for us, God, who is rich in mercy, made us alive with Christ" (Ephesians 2:1,4-5).

According to the Bible, all human beings have fallen from our Edenic perfection and now are sinners. But the Bible also teaches that heaven is a perfect place and no imperfect person will be allowed in. "Nothing impure will ever enter it" (Revelation 21:27). People who assume they will go to heaven when they die because they believe "I'm a pretty good person" will be eternally disappointed, to put it mildly. If God allowed them in, it would spoil heaven. The New Testament is clear: salvation is found only in Jesus.

On Thursdays, take time to pray for the salvation of those you love. There is no more eternally important prayer, and no finer display of love. Paul prayed for the salvation of his loved ones in Romans 10:1; we would be wise to follow his example.

A helmet, though, does more than just keep us alive; it also protects our minds and thoughts. This is why the Bible so often counsels us to be wise and think correctly, and it warns us that the pattern of our thoughts becomes the pattern of our lives: "For as he thinks within himself, so he is" (Proverbs 23:7 NASB). Plus, though we often mistakenly believe our thoughts are private, the Bible says otherwise: "The LORD knows all human plans," and "You have searched me, LORD, and you know me…you perceive my thoughts from afar" (Psalm 94:11; 139:1-2). We need to learn to "take captive every thought to make it obedient to Christ" (2 Corinthians 10:5). As Paul said elsewhere, "Whatever is true, whatever is noble, whatever is right, whatever is pure, whatever is lovely, whatever is admirable—if anything is excellent or praiseworthy—think about such things" (Philippians 4:8). In sum, we need to carefully guard our thought-lives.

There is so much to pray about on Thursdays, so many Scriptures to meditate upon, so many true, noble, right, pure, lovely, admirable thoughts and people to ponder…well, we could end up praying all day, which is what the Bible calls praying without ceasing. Learn to meditate on Scripture, for as G.K. Chesterton once said, "The object of opening the mind, as of opening the mouth, is to shut it again on something solid."[7]

And as we pray for God to enable us to think within the helmet of salvation, may God, in his power and grace, turn what usually is the devil's workshop into God's master studio.

Lord,

> Today is Thursday, so help me "think within the helmet of salvation."
>
> I am overflowing with thankfulness for your saving love, for my salvation was purchased at the high cost of the cross.
>
> I know there is no way I could ever earn or deserve salvation; salvation is by far the greatest gift I've ever been given.
>
> I pray for my family members to each come to saving faith.
>
> I pray for my friends and neighbors and coworkers to be saved.
>
> I pray for our church to be, not just a community of the saved, but a place in which people far from you will feel welcome and find grace.
>
> I pray that world leaders and peoples of all nations will be saved, and that Christians learn to take captive every thought to Christ.
>
> I pray this in the name of the one and only Savior, Jesus. Amen.

> > Colossians 2:7; Colossians 2:13-15; Titus 3:4-5; Romans 6:23; Luke 19:9; 1 Timothy 2:4; John 4:42; 1 Timothy 2:1-2; 2 Corinthians 10:5; Acts 4:12.

# FRIDAY

## Fight with the Sword of the Spirit

Thank God it's Friday!" is a well-known saying in our culture, and it's also the name of a national restaurant chain, TGI Fridays. For many Americans, this is because the dreaded workweek is almost over, and the weekend is about to begin. People who tend to be miserable Monday through Thursday suddenly perk up on Friday. It's time to par-tay!

I love the saying, "Thank God it's Friday!" I celebrate whenever our culture mentions God, and I love the reminder to give God our thanks. Plus, I love Fridays because that's the day to pray, "Fight with the sword of the Spirit."

### Why a Sword?

Most Bible readers quickly realize the first five pieces of the armor of God are designed for defense, not offense. Here, at last, we have an offensive weapon. "Take...the sword (*machaira*) of the Spirit, which is the word of God" (Ephesians 6:17). The Roman *machaira* was just under two feet long, double-edged, and extremely sharp. Its point came to "quite an obtuse angle,"[8] which gave the sword added strength, while also allowing it to penetrate enemy armor or flesh more efficiently.

The sword was important as a weapon for hand-to-hand combat. The Roman soldiers had other offensive weapons (including the javelins mentioned by Polybius), but Christians have only one offensive weapon, the

Word of God. This means our power is in the Word of God. This sword has the power to guide our lives, to direct our paths, to help us when in need, and to prevent us from making mistakes. The Bible, if we follow it, provides a moral rock upon which we can live our lives, a solid foundation for ourselves, our family, friendships, marriage, community, nation—everything.

Historically, the Bible was the moral rock upon which our nation was founded. This information may be overlooked in public classrooms today, but that doesn't change the fact that many of our national heroes believed the Bible was essential. George Washington said, "It is impossible to righteously govern the world without God and the Bible."[9] Andrew Jackson said, in reference to the Bible, "That book, sir, is the rock upon which our republic rests."[10] More recently, Ronald Reagan said, "Within the covers of one single book, the Bible, are all the answers to all the problems that face us today—if only we would read and believe."[11]

The problem is just that. Many people own a Bible, but they neither read it nor believe it. They certainly don't know its contents. As George Gallup said, "We live in a country of biblical illiterates."[12]

## Jesus' Use of the Sword of the Spirit

Jesus relied on the Scriptures profoundly, especially during his times of suffering. On the cross, Jesus quoted from Psalm 22:1: "My God, my God, why have you forsaken me?" (Matthew 27:46). Why would Jesus do this? Well, he had been raised in the synagogue, memorizing and praying the psalms, so in his time of need, he uttered a prayer he had learned. In the most excruciating moment of his life, the Scriptures gave voice to his deepest feelings. Jesus expressed his question to God and articulated his loneliness—in God's own words. I am in awe at such honesty, such brilliance, and such self-control. Think about it: when you stub a toe, do you say something you later regret or do you quote a perfectly pertinent Scripture?

When Jesus was challenged, he relied on and often quoted Scripture. For example, when the devil tempted Jesus three times, in each case he answered, "It is written…" (Matthew 4:1-11). Dear friend, this is how we are to fight against even the darkest evil: we turn on the light of God's Word. Jesus could have chosen to argue with the devil, but he did not. Instead, he used his powerful offensive weapon, the sword of the Spirit.

He had hidden God's Word in his heart, so he was ready and mightily equipped when the moment of battle came. His sword was well balanced and finely sharpened. He was ready for spiritual warfare.

This is the power of God's Word. As we privately study it week in and week out, as we go to church and listen to the Word of God preached, as we go to a home Bible study and devote ourselves to the apostles' teaching (Acts 2:42), and as we daily read the Scriptures to our children in our homes, God plants his Word in our hearts. Then, when the moment of battle comes, God will bring these Scriptures to mind, through the power of the Spirit, just when we need them.

## Why the Word of God?

In the Old Testament, God is a God who uses words. And because God is inherently powerful, his words are also inherently powerful. In Genesis 1, his words have the power to create reality from nothing. "And God said" was enough to create light, sky, dry ground, seas, and every living thing. Awesome.

In the New Testament, Jesus himself is the Word. "In the beginning was the Word, and the Word was with God, and the Word was God…The Word became flesh and made his dwelling among us" (John 1:1,14). In Jesus, God became flesh. Once again, we see that to put on the armor of God is to put on Christ. When we take up the Word of God, we do not become Bible-bashers who hit people over the head. No, to take up the sword of the Spirit is to clothe ourselves with Jesus, and let him and his words fight our battles. This imagery is especially vivid in the book of Revelation, in which Jesus is depicted with a sword coming out of his mouth (Revelation 1:16; 2:12,16) with which he fights those who follow the beast (Revelation 19:15,21).

My favorite Scripture about the power of God's Word, though, is by the unknown writer of Hebrews, who also likens it to a sword: "For the word of God is alive and active. Sharper than any double-edged sword, it penetrates even to dividing soul and spirit, joints and marrow; it judges the thoughts and attitudes of the heart" (Hebrews 4:12). God's Word is "alive and active"[13] because the Spirit of God is still moving through the written Scriptures. This is a dynamic understanding of the Word of God: it has the power to effect its own result.[14]

This is an incredibly marvelous truth, which an illustration from the world of computer technology might illuminate. The Word of God is inherently powerful, much like most computer programs today are self-installing. In the tortuous days of DOS, we laboriously had to install computer software on our own. Today, we merely put a new program disc in a computer (or click "download" on the Internet), and the program wonderfully self-installs (much to the delight of nontechies, like myself).

In a similar fashion, the Word of God is *self-installing*. Just reading and meditating on the Scriptures releases the inherent power of the Word of God, which gradually self-installs the will and wisdom of God into our lives. This is why it is so crucial that Christians and churches alike return to the practice of regular Scripture reading. The Word of God does not need to be made relevant; once it self-installs, it will effect its own relevance.

## Thank God It's Friday!

I love Fridays because I get to pray that my loved ones would be strong in the Word of God. Parents and grandparents, think about this for a moment. Would you like your children to grow up to be strong in the Word of God? What a terrific way to help put God's Word in their hearts and help them through all the storms of life, storms that may come even after we are dead and gone. Singles, would you like your friends and family to be strong in the Word of God? Pastors, would you like this for your congregants? How about for your neighbors, coworkers, or government leaders? I pray this whether they are believers or not—that they would come to value and follow the Word of God.

Are you ready to give those you love an offensive, spiritually powerful weapon? If so, pray the following prayer and help those you love win the battle.

Lord,

Today is Friday, so help me "fight with the sword of the Spirit."

I am so thankful for your Word, which is a mighty weapon, and also a source of peace and comfort.

Help me to become very familiar with your Word; put your precepts in both my mind and my heart.

I pray for my family members to love and trust your Word.

I pray my friends, neighbors, and coworkers will follow the Word.

I pray for our church to faithfully teach and live out the Word.

I pray that the leaders in our culture and nation would return to your Word, for without your counsel, no nation can prosper or last.

I pray this in the name of the living Word, Jesus. Amen.

> Hebrews 4:12; Psalm 119:52; Psalm 139:3; Job 22:22; Psalm 119:66; Psalm 119:63; Hebrews 5:12; Psalm 2:1; Revelation 1:18.

# SATURDAY

## Steadfastly Pray in the Spirit

Finally, after the Monday through Friday workweek, we come to Saturday. Hooray! Most people today love Saturdays, but that has not always been the case. Some ancients thought Saturday was an unlucky day. For instance, historian Daniel Boorstin wrote, "Among the Romans, Saturn's Day, or Saturday, was a day of evil omen when all tasks were ill-started, a day when battles should not be fought, nor journeys begun. No prudent person would want to risk the mishaps that Saturn might bring."[15]

In contrast, the biblical name for the last day of the week is Sabbath, or *Shabbat* in Hebrew, which literally means a day of "rest." I suggest that Saturday is a great day to rest in God in prayer.

### Why Prayer?

To this point we have learned how to pray the six pieces of the armor of God sequentially, Sunday through Friday. When I first began to do this, I noticed that the six pieces left Saturday open, so to speak. What was I to pray about on Saturday?

Then I noticed a key detail in Ephesians 6 that I had previously missed when preaching on the passage. The section did not end with the "sword of the Spirit," because "Spirit" is followed in Greek with a conjunction, rendered "and" in the NIV.

*And* pray in the Spirit on all occasions with all kinds of prayers and requests. With this in mind, be alert and always keep on praying for all the Lord's people. Pray also for me, that whenever I speak, words may be given me so that I will fearlessly make known the mystery of the gospel, for which I am an ambassador in chains. Pray that I may declare it fearlessly, as I should (Ephesians 6:18-20).

Paul says the last step in putting on the armor of God is *to keep praying about it*. Use all kinds of prayers, all sorts of requests, and pray for all types of people. After we pray for God to put his armor on us, we are to rest and put matters solidly in his hands. Will we be sufficiently protected from the evil one? Will any of the darts or arrows get through to injure us? Well, it's not our concern any longer. Following Paul's example, we trust God to take care of all things: "In all my prayers for all of you, I always pray with joy because of your partnership in the gospel from the first day until now, being confident of this, that he who began a good work in you will carry it on to completion until the day of Christ Jesus" (Philippians 1:4-6). We do all this through prayer.

What is prayer, after all? Christian prayer is not a strategy to gain favor or a way to punch our spiritual card in order to earn blessings. It's not a way to prove to God our sincerity, nor is it a way we merit rewards from him. It's not a duty we perform. It's not a work at all. So what is prayer? Prayer is the ultimate form of resting in God, which makes it a good match for the seventh day, the day of rest.

## Seven: A Revolution of Rest

Both *seven* and *rest* first appear in Genesis 2, at the end of God's creation week:

Thus the heavens and the earth were completed in all their vast array.

By the seventh day God had finished the work he had been doing; so on the seventh (*shebay*) day he rested (*shabath*) from all his work. Then God blessed the seventh day and made it holy, because on it he rested from all the work of creating that he had done (Genesis 2:1-3).

In Hebrew there is a slight play on words between "seventh" and "rest." If you will pardon my mixed translation: "On the *shebay*(th) day God *shabath*(ed)." In fact, both words are derivatives of the same Hebrew root *shaba*, which meant "to be complete." This is why, biblically, seven is the perfect or complete number, and why seven can also indicate divinity.

As a result, most Bible students and religion scholars recognize seven as a number with spiritual significance; seven had theological weight, if you will. This explains a factoid that many people don't know: "seven" was also how the ancient Hebrews swore. When King Abimelech asked Abraham to agree to a treaty by taking a solemn oath, Abraham said, literally in Hebrew, "I *seven* it" (Genesis 21:24). Most English translations render this verse, "I swear it," thereby losing the colorful, numerical meaning. Plus, even God did this. To the kings of Judah, he said, "If you do not obey these commands, I *seven* myself that this palace will become a ruin" (Jeremiah 22:5). In other words, this oath was as true as if one were to repeat oneself seven times.

So seven is an amazing number in the Bible, and conveys several important meanings in addition to its numerical meaning. But the most revolutionary historical fact about the Hebrew seven is that time began to be measured in seven-day weeks.

Today, the concept that time is divided into weeks with seven days is a worldwide norm. But this was not so in the ancient world. Most cultures followed a lunar calendar, which turned over roughly every thirty days.[16] The Babylonians followed a calendar based on the number six (which was also the basis of their numerical system, hence 666 as the sign of the beast), and the Mayans had twenty-day months. The Romans had an eight-day week, whereas the Greeks apparently had no week. Cultures had at least "fifteen different ways, in bunches of five to ten days each, of clustering their days together."[17] There just was, and is, no simple way to evenly divide our solar year and lunar months.

The point is this: the only justification for our seven-day week, which we all are so familiar with, is a spiritual one. Because of this, when France tried to secularize its society in the late 1700s, the leaders realized that a seven-day week was wholly a religious idea. Consequently, the new government jettisoned the seven-day system and imposed a calendar with ten days per week. However, the new calendar was a massive failure and was abandoned after only a few years.

So why did God reveal to the Hebrews that seven days would comprise a week? Sure, God worked for six days and then rested on the seventh, and the fourth of the Ten Commandments specified, "Observe the Sabbath day by keeping it holy...On [the seventh day] you shall not do any work" (Deuteronomy 5:12,14). But why seven? After all, our calendars would have been simpler had God chosen the tenth day. The reason goes back to the relation of seven (*shebay*) to rest (*shaboth*). Here is the Copernican revolution the Hebrews brought to the world: humans should *rest* at regular intervals. God modeled this in his own creation activity, and he wants us to follow suit.

But we humans are notorious workaholics, and even when we have enough, we tend to want more. In human history before this revelation, people worked 24/7. In preindustrial cultures, there was always more work to do. Free people and children, slaves and animals, everyone worked. Unless people were of royal lineage, they worked from sunup until sundown all life long. This is one reason, in addition to disease and war, that life expectancy was so short: people simply wore out earlier as the nonstop hard work took its toll.

Thomas Cahill wrote in *The Gift of the Jews*, "No ancient society before the Jews had a day of rest. The God who made the universe and rested bids us do the same, calling us to a weekly restoration of prayer, study, and recreation (or re-creation)...The Sabbath is surely one of the simplest and sanest recommendations any god has ever made."[18]

So God established the Sabbath and told humans to make it holy— by resting. It's okay to relax, to put your feet up, and take a break once in a while. In short, rest is a spiritual activity.

## Why Pray on Saturday?

If to pray is to rest, to put our concerns in the hands of God and leave them there, then what better day could there be for prayer than Saturday?

The Bible is full of promises of rest, and Jesus himself lived a life of restful trust in his Father. In fact, one of Jesus' final statements, uttered just before his death, was, "Father, into your hands I commit my spirit" (Luke 23:46). What a finale: the one who lived in constant communion with his Father ended his life with a prayer of *shaboth*, a prayer of rest and trust in his *Abba*.

We can do the same, knowing that our eternal rest is in good hands. Like a flourish at the end of a bravado performance, the Bible ends with the realities of life after death, which divides clearly into those that will never rest and those who will be given never-ending rest. Concerning the former, the Bible alarmingly says,

> And the smoke of their torment will rise for ever and ever. There will be no rest day or night for those who worship the beast and its image, or for anyone who receives the mark of its name (Revelation 14:11).

Fortunately, the opposite is true for believers:

> Then I heard a voice from heaven say, "Write this: Blessed are the dead who die in the Lord from now on."

> "Yes," says the Spirit, "they will rest from their labor, for their deeds will follow them" (Revelation 14:13).

So, dear friends, prayerfully be at rest, both now and forevermore (Psalm 23:6).

*Rest.*

Repose in the love of the Father, the grace of the Son, and the comfort of the Spirit (1 John 3:1; 1 Thessalonians 5:28; John 14:16; 2 Corinthians 1:3-4).

*Be still.*

Pray that your soul would be quiet and at rest, like a weaned child with its mother (Psalm 131:2).

*Selah.*

Pray for the rest that Jesus promised to give (Matthew 11:28).

*Be quiet.*

Rest in the protective armor of God (Psalm 34:7).
*Relax.*
Pray for God's rest upon your soul (Ephesians 6:18; Hebrews 4:1-11).
*Shalom.*

Lord,

> The week is now over, and on this Saturday I ask you to help me "steadfastly pray in the Spirit."
>
> Help me pray in the Spirit on all occasions, with all kinds of prayers and requests.
>
> Help me to be alert and keep praying for all your people.
>
> I pray that you create in my family members a love for prayer.
>
> I pray that our church would be a house of prayer.
>
> I pray that our business, community, and government leaders would humble themselves before you in prayer.
>
> Help us seek your face, so you will heal our land.
>
> In the name of the One in whom we rest. Amen.

> Ephesians 6:18; Philippians 4:6; Colossians 1:3; Psalm 42:8; Matthew 21:13; James 4:10; 2 Chronicles 7:14.

# PART TWO

Prayer Guides for Praying
the Armor of God Daily

# Instructions for
## Using the Daily Prayer Guides

The rest of this book contains ten weeks of daily prayers, which provide guides to practice and learn the "Praying the Armor of God" method. Each day follows a simple pattern:

- First, we begin each day by recording the date and the name of the person(s) we are praying for.

- Second, we pray at least two Scriptures, which are provided to ground the prayer in God's Word and in that day's theme.

- Third, a "daily prayer opener" helps remind us of the reality of spiritual warfare and of our need to pray the armor of God.

- Fourth, an "armor prayer" guides us through each day's piece of armor.

These prayers are thoroughly based upon and infused with Scripture, so as we follow this guide, we literally are praying Scripture. When we pray God's Word, we speak God's promises and truths back to him. A wise pastor once told me, "Rick, make sure you have lots of Scripture in your sermons, because that's the only part you can be sure is absolutely true." In the same way, praying God's words back to him gives us confidence that the words we are praying are accurate and true.

In addition, praying Scripture helps solve a practical problem for many Christians: the tendency to pray the same few words and phrases over and over. Have you ever felt uncomfortable praying in public because you just didn't have the right words to say? Or have you tried to pray but soon ran out of words or topics? If you answered yes to either question, you are not alone. But help is at hand. As you pray through this guide, week after week and month after month, you will gradually develop a deeper vocabulary and phraseology of prayer, which over time will produce a richer and more vibrant prayer life.

Also, don't be afraid of repetition in prayer. In the prayers that follow, I suggest that you begin each day with similar prayer openers, and over the course of the ten weeks, you will repeat other phrases many times. This too is biblical (check out Psalm 136), and aids in memory retention.

## Flexibility in Prayer

As you pray, remember to enjoy the process. Have fun. Try to pray these with a smile on your face and joy in your heart. Don't take yourself, the structure, or the schedule too seriously. Feel free to adjust the pace and prayers as needed; in Christ we are free indeed (John 8:36). Rigidity in prayer produces prayer Pharisees, while elasticity in prayer produces seasoned and servant-hearted prayer warriors.

For instance, you may find some of the weeks especially meaningful, and decide to linger and pray them, over and over, for several weeks. On the other hand, if you find that a week's topic doesn't apply at all, feel free to skip it. Or if you have a large family (or group of friends), you may find it difficult to pray a certain day's prayer for each person by name. It just takes too much time. But there's no hurry, so you may choose to repeat a certain prayer or set of prayers for several days or weeks, selecting just a few family members to pray for at a time.

When the ten weeks are completed, you can start over again from the beginning...and again...and again.

In time, as you adapt these prayers to the issues pressing on your heart, the rhythm of your life, and the tone of your words, you will find that you are less tied to the pages of this book. Then, these prayers will begin to spontaneously arise in your spirit at unexpected times throughout the day, almost like a background program working on a computer. In my own life, daily praying the armor of God provides a theme I can focus on each day, which results in what the Bible calls "continual prayer" (1 Thessalonians 5:17).

On Sundays, for instance, I find that truth becomes the focus of my day and prayers. As I pass people in the halls at church, I pray for the belt of truth in their lives. As I sit with my wife or miss my kids who are away at college, I pray for God's truth to be the bedrock of their lives. As I drive through town and see apartments or houses, I pray for those families to discover the truth about God's existence and love. As I drive by other buildings, I pray for churches to be girded with God's truth, for businesses to operate honestly, and for government to serve with integrity. As I watch the evening news, I silently pray for God's truth to penetrate and transform the people, the communities, and the nations in the news. And as I lie in bed at night, I thank God for his truth, which has transformed my life and has brought so many blessings. Actually, it's pretty easy to pray continually because the impact of God's truth is so wonderful, and because there are so many people in our world who need their eyes opened to God's truth.

To jump-start this process, I suggest that you bookmark each day's page, carry this book with you, and pray these prayers whenever you have a few spare moments. Or take a picture of the day's prayers with your smartphone or tablet device, and set your alarm to remind you to pray several times a day. Praying repeatedly will help saturate your mind, heart, and soul with the armor of God.

## Praying Aloud

As you begin the daily adventure of praying the armor of God, I encourage you to pray the Scriptures and prayers *aloud*. There is something special about voicing our prayers that embeds them into our memory, which is exactly what we want in praying Scripture: to hide God's Word in our hearts (Psalm 119:11). As we speak or softly whisper these prayers, the scriptural phrases gradually become part of our prayer vocabulary. To vocalize a word better imprints it upon our minds, which is why memory experts say it's handy to repeat the names of people we meet for the first time. If we quickly say their names out loud two or three times in the first sentences we share, we will be much more likely to remember those names. Try it—it works.

Plus, praying aloud actually has its root in Scripture. One of the main Hebrew words for "meditate" is *haggah*, which literally means "to mumble, murmur, or mutter." It clearly is an onomatopoetic word, a term that sounds like its action. Other examples are the *buzz* of a bee, the *bark* of a dog, and the *bang* of a gun. When we meditate by reading the words of Scripture softly aloud, to others around us it may sound like we are saying, "*haggah-haggah-haggah*" or "*mumble-mumble-mumble.*" This is what the Orthodox Jews to this day do at the Wailing Wall in Jerusalem: they meditate on Scripture, which means that they prayerfully read it aloud, albeit quietly.

Meditating on Scripture, in this fashion, takes charge of our minds and guides our thought lives. Because of this, biblical meditation can help us conquer worry and fear. Let's admit it: many of us are plagued with worries and concerns that can dominate our thought lives even while we go about our normal activities. We can be at work doing our jobs, at a store shopping, or at church listening to a sermon, but in our minds, we are worrying and fretting about something. We might be driving our cars or lying in bed trying to fall asleep, but our minds cannot stop themselves from the constant *grumble-grumble-grumble.*

The solution is to meditate, to *haggah* Scripture, which is to repeat a Scripture or a Scripture-based prayer over and over. Thus Christian meditation is a form of prayer, and it is very different from the meditation practiced in some Eastern religions, such as Buddhism or Hinduism. Eastern meditation seeks to empty the mind by repeating a meaningless phrase, a mantra. Christian meditation does the exact opposite: it fills the mind with a meaningful phrase. Praying replaces our worry-thoughts with worship-thoughts; it gets our minds off the bad and onto the good. And if the worry is an especially stubborn one, softly praying aloud is an extra boost to displace our negative thoughts.

Bottom line, we can either pray or worry, mumble or grumble, meditate or be miserable—and all are forms of *haggah.* In Psalm 1:2, for instance, we are blessed if we meditate (*haggah*) on the Law day and night. Conversely, in Psalm 2:1 the psalmist asks, "Why do the nations conspire and the peoples plot (*haggah*) in vain?" Our lives are dominated by thoughts that are either positive or negative, good or bad, honoring to God or to the enemy. Daily praying the armor of God can help us win the battle in our minds.

We are trained to read silently, so this may be difficult for you at first.

You will be tempted to read both the opening Scriptures and the prayers silently. It will greatly enhance your prayer experience if you read them audibly. Give it a try!

## Daily Prayer Openers

Here's one final piece of advice before we start: I encourage you to memorize and start each day's prayer with a little prayer opener. It's a great habit to establish. We brush our teeth to start our day, fasten our seat belts when we get into cars, and say "Love ya!" at the end of a phone call with a family member. Over time, these habits become automatic and thereby help us live better lives.

The same can be true of a daily prayer opener, and I've included a couple of examples, one for ourselves and one for others, in the following pages. You might dog-ear those pages (manually or digitally) so you can refer to these prayers easily later. Or you can copy them to a scrap of paper that can serve as a bookmark as you travel from day to day on this prayer journey.

My hope is that you will memorize this daily prayer opener (or some form of it) during the first weeks, and it will gradually morph and take on your own personality, words, and shape. The important point is to pray this every day of the week, for yourself and those you love, in order to position yourself correctly to pray the armor of God. It reminds us that spiritual warfare is not something we can fight on our own power, and the pieces of the armor of God are not items we can make for ourselves.

Let's give it a try. Turn to the next page, and pray these Scriptures and daily prayer openers softly aloud (you don't need to recite the Scripture references; they are provided for your further study).

## Daily Prayer Openers

### Scriptures

*Lord, your Word teaches…*

> Be alert and of sober mind. Your enemy the devil prowls around like a roaring lion looking for someone to devour (1 Peter 5:8).

> Put on the full armor of God, so that you can take your stand against the devil's schemes (Ephesians 6:11).

### Daily Prayer Opener (for ourselves)

Lord,

I am not strong enough to fight the evil one.

If I try to fight the devil with my own strength, I will fail completely.

Instead, I ask you to strengthen me, Lord, with your mighty power.

As I understand the need for physical protection, help me grasp my need for spiritual protection.

I ask you to put on me the very character of Christ, because it's light that overcomes darkness.

I ask you to put on me your full armor, O God, so I can take my stand against the devil's schemes.

In the name of Jesus I pray. Amen.

> Luke 22:31-32; 2 Chronicles 20:12; 2 Chronicles 16:9; Ephesians 1:19; 1 Samuel 17:38; Romans 13:14; John 1:5; Ephesians 6:11.

Next, pray the same prayer aloud for someone you love:

## Daily Prayer Opener (for others)

Lord,

My wife (husband, child, parent), _____ (insert name), is not strong enough to fight the evil one.

If she (he) tries to fight the devil with her (his) own strength, she (he) will fail completely.

Instead, I ask you to strengthen her (him), Lord, with your mighty power.

As she (he) understands the need for physical protection, help her (him) grasp her (his) need for spiritual protection.

I ask you to put on her (him) the very character of Christ, because it's light that overcomes darkness.

I ask you to put on her (him) your full armor, O God, so she (he) can take her (his) stand against the devil's schemes.

In the name of Jesus I pray. Amen.

> Luke 22:31-32; 2 Chronicles 20:12; Ephesians 1:19; 1 Samuel 17:38; 2 Chronicles 16:9; Psalm 3:3; Romans 13:14; John 1:5; Ephesians 6:11.

# WEEK ONE

## Starting to Pray the Armor of God

### Instructions for Week One

This week we will learn how to pray the armor of God for ourselves. At first this may seem a bit selfish, but it will help us get the flow of praying the armor of God daily, which we can then build on in the weeks to come. Next week we will add a few family members, and in week five we will pray for close friends. Later weeks will introduce new prayers with varying degrees of complexity.

Let's begin by recording today's date, and then praying the Scriptures and prayers aloud.

### SUNDAY: Strap on the Belt of Truth

*Lord, today I enter your presence and pray for myself:*

Date: _____

(Use the following spaces for future weeks when you cycle again through these prayers.)

Date: _____ Date: _____ Date: _____ Date: _____

Date: _____ Date: _____ Date: _____ Date: _____

## Scriptures

*Lord, your Word teaches...*

> Stand firm then, with the belt of truth buckled around your waist (Ephesians 6:14).

> "I am the way and the truth and the life" (John 14:6).

## Daily Prayer Opener

Lord,

I'm not strong enough to fight the evil one.

If I try to fight the devil with my own strength, I will fail completely.

Instead, I ask you to strengthen me, Lord, with your mighty power.

As I understand the need for physical protection, help me grasp my need for spiritual protection.

I ask you to put on me the very character of Christ, because it's light that overcomes darkness.

I ask you to put on me your full armor, O God, so I can take my stand against the devil's schemes. Amen.

> Luke 22:31-32; 2 Chronicles 20:12; 2 Chronicles 16:9; Ephesians 1:19; 1 Samuel 17:38; Psalm 3:3; Romans 13:14; John 1:5; Ephesians 6:11.

## Armor Prayer

Lord,

It's Sunday, so it's a great opportunity to "strap on the belt of truth."

This world is filled with lies and liars, and I don't want to be one of them!

I want to be like Jesus, who is the way, the truth and the life, but every time I try to be like Jesus, I fall short.

So Lord, I ask you today to put on me the belt of truth, and clothe me with Jesus himself.

Allow the truthfulness of Jesus to live in and through me today, and may the light of Jesus shine through my life! Amen.

John 8:44; John 14:6; Romans 13:14.

## MONDAY: Make Fast the Breastplate of Righteousness

*Lord, today I enter your presence and pray for myself:*

Date: _____ Date: _____ Date: _____ Date: _____

Date: _____ Date: _____ Date: _____ Date: _____

### Scriptures

*Lord, your Word teaches...*

> Stand firm then...with the breastplate of righteousness in place (Ephesians 6:14).

> Those who are wise will shine like the brightness of the heavens, and those who lead many to righteousness, like the stars for ever and ever (Daniel 12:3).

### Daily Prayer Opener

Lord,

I'm not strong enough to fight the evil one.

If I try to fight the devil with my own strength, I will fail completely.

Instead, I ask you to strengthen me, Lord, with your mighty power.

As I understand the need for physical protection, help me grasp my need for spiritual protection.

I ask you to put on me the very character of Christ, because it's light that overcomes darkness.

I ask you to put on me your full armor, O God, so I can take my stand against the devil's schemes. Amen.

> Luke 22:31-32; 2 Chronicles 20:12; 2 Chronicles 16:9; Ephesians 1:19; 1 Samuel 17:38; Psalm 3:3; Romans 13:14; John 1:5; Ephesians 6:11.

## Armor Prayer

Lord,

I pray on this Monday that you "make fast upon me the breastplate of righteousness" to protect my heart from the evil one.

I pray that you keep me pure and holy in a world that is neither, for this world is filled with filth and corruption, and people today seem to have no sense of shame.

I want to be like Jesus, who is the Holy One, but every time I try to be like Jesus, I fall short.

So Lord, I ask you today to fill me with your holiness and purity, and clothe me with Jesus himself.

Allow the righteousness of Jesus to live in and through me today, and may the light of Jesus shine through my life! Amen.

> Zephaniah 3:5; Luke 1:35; Romans 13:14.

## TUESDAY: Tread in the Shoes of Peace

*Lord, today I enter your presence and pray for myself:*

Date: _____ Date: _____ Date: _____ Date: _____

Date: _____ Date: _____ Date: _____ Date: _____

## Scriptures

*Lord, your Word teaches...*

> Stand firm then...with your feet fitted with the readiness that comes from the gospel of peace (Ephesians 6:14-15).

> Peacemakers who sow in peace reap a harvest of righteousness (James 3:18).

## Daily Prayer Opener

Lord,

I'm not strong enough to fight the evil one.

If I try to fight the devil with my own strength, I will fail completely.

Instead, I ask you to strengthen me, Lord, with your mighty power.

As I understand the need for physical protection, help me grasp my need for spiritual protection.

I ask you to put on me the very character of Christ, because it's light that overcomes darkness.

I ask you to put on me your full armor, O God, so I can take my stand against the devil's schemes. Amen.

> Luke 22:31-32; 2 Chronicles 20:12; 2 Chronicles 16:9; Ephesians 1:19; 1 Samuel 17:38; Psalm 3:3; Romans 13:14; John 1:5; Ephesians 6:11.

## Armor Prayer

Lord,

I pray on this Tuesday that you help me "tread in the shoes of peace."

This world is filled with wars and rumors of war, and relationships are filled with conflict and struggle.

I want to be like Jesus, who is the Prince of Peace, but every time I
  try to be like Jesus, I fall short.

So Lord, I ask you today to put on me the shoes of peace.

Clothe me with Jesus himself, and help me become a peacemaker
  and conflict-resolver.

Allow the healing peace of Jesus to live in and through me today,
  and may the light of Jesus shine through my life! Amen.

Matthew 24:6; Isaiah 9:6; Romans 13:14.

## WEDNESDAY: Wield the Shield of Faith

*Lord, today I enter your presence and pray for myself:*

Date: _____ Date: _____ Date: _____ Date: _____

Date: _____ Date: _____ Date: _____ Date: _____

## Scriptures

*Lord, your Word teaches…*

> Stand firm then…[and] take up the shield of faith, with
> which you can extinguish all the flaming arrows of the evil
> one (Ephesians 6:14,16).

> Without faith it is impossible to please God (Hebrews 11:6).

## Daily Prayer Opener

Lord,

I'm not strong enough to fight the evil one.

If I try to fight the devil with my own strength, I will fail
  completely.

Instead, I ask you to strengthen me, Lord, with your mighty power.

As I understand the need for physical protection, help me grasp my need for spiritual protection.

I ask you to put on me the very character of Christ, because it's light that overcomes darkness.

I ask you to put on me your full armor, O God, so I can take my stand against the devil's schemes. Amen.

> Luke 22:31-32; 2 Chronicles 20:12; 2 Chronicles 16:9; Ephesians 1:19; 1 Samuel 17:38; Psalm 3:3; Romans 13:14; John 1:5; Ephesians 6:11.

## Armor Prayer

Lord,

It's Wednesday, so I ask you to help me "wield the shield of faith."

This world is filled with doubters and skeptics, and I don't want to be one of them.

I want to be like Jesus, who is the Faithful One, but every time I try to be like Jesus, I fall short.

So Lord, I ask you today to put on me the shield of faith, and clothe me with Jesus himself.

Allow the faith, hope, and trust of Jesus to live in and through me today, and may the light of Jesus shine through my life! Amen.

> John 8:44; Revelation 19:11; Romans 13:14.

## THURSDAY: Think Within the Helmet of Salvation

*Lord, today I enter your presence and pray for myself:*

Date: _____ Date: _____ Date: _____ Date: _____

Date: _____ Date: _____ Date: _____ Date: _____

## Scriptures

*Lord, your Word teaches…*

> Stand firm then…Take the helmet of salvation (Ephesians 6:14,17).

> Sing to the LORD, all the earth;
>    proclaim his salvation day after day.
>                        (1 Chronicles 16:23)

## Daily Prayer Opener

Lord,

I'm not strong enough to fight the evil one.

If I try to fight the devil with my own strength, I will fail completely.

Instead, I ask you to strengthen me, Lord, with your mighty power.

As I understand the need for physical protection, help me grasp my need for spiritual protection.

I ask you to put on me the very character of Christ, because it's light that overcomes darkness.

I ask you to put on me your full armor, O God, so I can take my stand against the devil's schemes. Amen.

> Luke 22:31-32; 2 Chronicles 20:12; 2 Chronicles 16:9; Ephesians 1:19; 1 Samuel 17:38; Psalm 3:3; Romans 13:14; John 1:5; Ephesians 6:11.

## Armor Prayer

Lord,

Today is Thursday, so help me "think within the helmet of salvation."

People today are so independent and self-assured; they even believe they will go to heaven when they die because they consider themselves to be "pretty good" people.

How surprised they will be on the day of judgment when they learn that heaven is a perfect place where nothing impure can enter.

What a shock that will be—and I don't want to be one of them!

I thank you for Jesus, whose name is the only name by which I can be saved.

So Lord, I ask you today to put on me the helmet of salvation and clothe me with Jesus himself.

Allow the saving grace of Jesus to live in and through me, and may the light of Jesus shine through my life! Amen.

Revelation 21:27; Acts 4:12; Romans 13:14.

## FRIDAY: Fight with the Sword of the Spirit

*Lord, today I enter your presence and pray for myself:*

Date: _____ Date: _____ Date: _____ Date: _____

Date: _____ Date: _____ Date: _____ Date: _____

## Scriptures

*Lord, your Word teaches…*

Stand firm then…Take the sword of the Spirit, which is the word of God (Ephesians 6:14,17).

> Your word, LORD, is eternal;
>    it stands firm in the heavens.
>                               (Psalm 119:89)

## Daily Prayer Opener

Lord,

I'm not strong enough to fight the evil one.

If I try to fight the devil with my own strength, I will fail completely.

Instead, I ask you to strengthen me, Lord, with your mighty power.

As I understand the need for physical protection, help me grasp my need for spiritual protection.

I ask you to put on me the very character of Christ, because it's light that overcomes darkness.

I ask you to put on me your full armor, O God, so I can take my stand against the devil's schemes. Amen.

> Luke 22:31-32; 2 Chronicles 20:12; 2 Chronicles 16:9; Ephesians 1:19; 1 Samuel 17:38; Psalm 3:3; Romans 13:14; John 1:5; Ephesians 6:11.

## Armor Prayer

Lord,

Today is Friday, so help me "fight with the sword of the Spirit."

This world is filled with opinions and theories, and people are so convinced their own way is best, they think they can even redefine words and morals.

Lord, I don't want to be one of them!

I want your Word to guide my path, fill my mind, comfort my heart, and flow from my lips.

I want to be like Jesus, who is the Word of God, and who defeated
the enemy with Scripture.

So Lord, I ask you to arm me with the sword of the Spirit, which is
to clothe me with Jesus himself.

Allow the Word of God to live in and through me today, and may
the light of Jesus shine through my life! Amen.

John 1:1; Romans 13:14.

## SATURDAY: Steadfastly Pray in the Spirit

*Lord, today I enter your presence and pray for myself:*

Date: _____ Date: _____ Date: _____ Date: _____

Date: _____ Date: _____ Date: _____ Date: _____

## Scriptures

*Lord, your Word teaches...*

Stand firm then...And pray in the Spirit on all occasions
with all kinds of prayers and requests. With this in mind,
be alert and always keep on praying for all the Lord's people
(Ephesians 6:14,18).

Then Jesus told his disciples a parable to show them that
they should always pray and not give up (Luke 18:1).

## Daily Prayer Opener

Lord,

I'm not strong enough to fight the evil one.

If I try to fight the devil with my own strength, I will fail
completely.

Instead, I ask you to strengthen me, Lord, with your mighty power.

As I understand the need for physical protection, help me grasp my need for spiritual protection.

I ask you to put on me the very character of Christ, because it's light that overcomes darkness.

I ask you to put on me your full armor, O God, so I can take my stand against the devil's schemes. Amen.

> Luke 22:31-32; 2 Chronicles 20:12; 2 Chronicles 16:9; Ephesians 1:19; 1 Samuel 17:38; Psalm 3:3; Romans 13:14; John 1:5; Ephesians 6:11.

## Armor Prayer

Lord,

The week is now over, and on this Saturday I ask you to help me "steadfastly pray in the Spirit."

This world is filled with people who doubt the power of prayer, and I don't want to be one of them.

I want to be like Jesus, who took time out of his busy schedule to pray, who taught his followers to pray, and who prayerfully sought his Father in his hour of need.

But every time I try to be like Jesus, I fall short.

So Lord, I ask you today to fill me with the prayerfulness of Jesus, clothe me with Jesus himself.

Allow Jesus to live in and through me today as I pray without ceasing, and may the light of Jesus shine through my life! Amen.

> Mark 1:35; Luke 11:1-13; Luke 22:39-46; Romans 13:14.

# WEEK TWO

# Learning to Pray for Our Families

### Instructions for Week Two

This week we will learn how to pray the armor of God for others. We will start by praying the Daily Prayer Opener and the Armor Prayer for a specific family member (these prayers are just adaptations from week one to train us how to modify a prayer for ourselves into a prayer for others). Then we can pray these again for one or two other family members.

## SUNDAY: Strap on the Belt of Truth

*Lord, today I bow before you in prayer for these family members:*

Date: _____ Names: _____

(Use the following spaces for future weeks when you cycle again through these prayers.)

Date: _____ Names: _____

Date: _____ Names: _____

Date: _____ Names: _____

## Scriptures

*Lord, your Word teaches…*

> Stand firm then, with the belt of truth buckled around your waist (Ephesians 6:14).

> To them God has chosen to make known among the Gentiles the glorious riches of this mystery, which is Christ in you, the hope of glory (Colossians 1:27).

## Daily Prayer Opener

Lord,

My husband (wife, child, parent, brother, sister), _____ (insert name), is not strong enough to fight the evil one.

If he (she) tries to fight the devil with his (her) own strength, he (she) will fail completely.

Instead, I ask you to strengthen him (her), Lord, with your mighty power.

As he (she) understands the need for physical protection, help him (her) grasp his (her) need for spiritual protection.

I ask you to put on him (her) the very character of Christ, because it's light that overcomes darkness.

I ask you to put on him (her) your full armor, O God, so he (she) can take his (her) stand against the devil's schemes. Amen.

> Luke 22:31-32; 2 Chronicles 20:12; 2 Chronicles 16:9; Ephesians 1:19; 1 Samuel 17:38; Psalm 3:3; Romans 13:14; John 1:5; Ephesians 6:11.

## Armor Prayer

Lord,

It's Sunday, so it's a great opportunity to "strap on the belt of truth," so I pray that you would gird your truth around _____ (insert name).

This world is filled with lies and liars, and I don't want him (her) to be one of them.

I want him (her) to be like Jesus, who is the way, the truth, and the life, but I also realize that if he (she) tries to be truthful, he (she) will fall short.

So Lord, I ask you today to put on him (her) the belt of truth, and clothe him (her) with Jesus himself.

Allow the truthfulness of Jesus to live in and through him (her) today, and may the light of Jesus shine through his (her) life! Amen.

John 8:44; John 14:6; Romans 13:14.

## MONDAY: Make Fast the Breastplate of Righteousness

*Lord, today I bow before you in prayer for these family members:*

Date: _____ Names: _____

Date: _____ Names: _____

Date: _____ Names: _____

Date: _____ Names: _____

## Scriptures

*Lord, your Word teaches…*

Stand firm then…with the breastplate of righteousness in place (Ephesians 6:14).

I will give thanks to the LORD because of his righteousness;
I will sing the praises of the name of the LORD Most High.
(Psalm 7:17)

## Daily Prayer Opener

Lord,

My husband (wife, child, parent, brother, sister), _____ (insert name), is not strong enough to fight the evil one.

If he (she) tries to fight the devil with his (her) own strength, he (she) will fail completely.

Instead, I ask you to strengthen him (her), Lord, with your mighty power.

As he (she) understands the need for physical protection, help him (her) grasp his (her) need for spiritual protection.

I ask you to put on him (her) the very character of Christ, because it's light that overcomes darkness.

I ask you to put on him (her) your full armor, O God, so he (she) can take his (her) stand against the devil's schemes. Amen.

> Luke 22:31-32; 2 Chronicles 20:12; 2 Chronicles 16:9; Ephesians 1:19; 1 Samuel 17:38; Psalm 3:3; Romans 13:14; John 1:5; Ephesians 6:11.

## Armor Prayer

Lord,

I pray on this Monday that you make fast upon _____ (insert name) the breastplate of righteousness, to protect her (his) heart from the evil one.

I pray that you keep her (him) pure and holy in a world that is neither, for this world is filled with filth and corruption, and people today seem to have no sense of shame.

I pray for her (him) to become more like Jesus, who is the Holy One, but I also realize that if she (he) tries to be holy, she (he) will fall short.

So Lord, I ask you today to fill her (him) with your holiness and purity, and clothe her (him) with Jesus himself.

Allow the righteousness of Jesus to live in and through her (him) today, and may the light of Jesus shine through her (his) life! Amen.

Zephaniah 3:5; Luke 1:35; Romans 13:14.

## TUESDAY: Tread in the Shoes of Peace

*Lord, today I bow before you in prayer for these family members:*

Date: _____ Names: _____

Date: _____ Names: _____

Date: _____ Names: _____

Date: _____ Names: _____

## Scriptures

*Lord, your Word teaches...*

> Stand firm then...with your feet fitted with the readiness that comes from the gospel of peace (Ephesians 6:14-15).

> The LORD gives strength to his people;
> the LORD blesses his people with peace.
> (Psalm 29:11)

## Daily Prayer Opener

Lord,

My husband (wife, child, parent, brother, sister), _____ (insert name), is not strong enough to fight the evil one.

If he (she) tries to fight the devil with his (her) own strength, he (she) will fail completely.

Instead, I ask you to strengthen him (her), Lord, with your mighty power.

As he (she) understands the need for physical protection, help him (her) grasp his (her) need for spiritual protection.

I ask you to put on him (her) the very character of Christ, because it's light that overcomes darkness.

I ask you to put on him (her) your full armor, O God, so he (she) can take his (her) stand against the devil's schemes. Amen.

> Luke 22:31-32; 2 Chronicles 20:12; 2 Chronicles 16:9; Ephesians 1:19; 1 Samuel 17:38; Psalm 3:3; Romans 13:14; John 1:5; Ephesians 6:11.

## Armor Prayer

Lord,

I pray on this Tuesday that you help _____ (insert name), "tread in the shoes of peace."

This world is filled with wars and rumors of war, and relationships are filled with conflict and struggle.

I want him (her) to be like Jesus, who is the Prince of Peace, but every time he (she) tries to be like Jesus, he (she) will fall short.

So Lord, I ask you today to put on him (her) the shoes of peace.

Clothe him (her) with Jesus himself, and help him (her) become a peacemaker and conflict-resolver.

Allow the healing peace of Jesus to live in and through him (her) today, and may the light of Jesus shine through his (her) life! Amen.

> Matthew 24:6; Isaiah 9:6; Romans 13:14.

## WEDNESDAY: Wield the Shield of Faith

*Lord, today I bow before you in prayer for these family members:*

Date: _____ Names: _____

Date: _____ Names: _____

Date: _____ Names: _____

Date: _____ Names: _____

### Scriptures

*Lord, your Word teaches…*

> Stand firm then…[and] take up the shield of faith, with
> which you can extinguish all the flaming arrows of the evil
> one (Ephesians 6:14,16).

> Because of the LORD's great love we are not consumed,
>     for his compassions never fail.
> They are new every morning;
>     great is your faithfulness.
>                                    (Lamentations 3:22-23)

### Daily Prayer Opener

Lord,

My husband (wife, child, parent, brother, sister), _____
    (insert name), is not strong enough to fight the evil one.

If he (she) tries to fight the devil with his (her) own strength, he
    (she) will fail completely.

Instead, I ask you to strengthen him (her), Lord, with your mighty
    power.

As he (she) understands the need for physical protection, help him
    (her) grasp his (her) need for spiritual protection.

I ask you to put on him (her) the very character of Christ, because it's light that overcomes darkness.

I ask you to put on him (her) your full armor, O God, so he (she) can take his (her) stand against the devil's schemes. Amen.

> Luke 22:31-32; 2 Chronicles 20:12; 2 Chronicles 16:9; Ephesians 1:19; 1 Samuel 17:38; Psalm 3:3; Romans 13:14; John 1:5; Ephesians 6:11.

## Armor Prayer

Lord,

It's Wednesday, so I ask you to help _____ (insert name), "wield the shield of faith."

This world is filled with doubters and skeptics, and I don't want her (him) to be one of them.

I want her (him) to be like Jesus, who is the Faithful One, but every time she (he) tries to be like Jesus, she (he) will fall short.

So Lord, I ask you today to put on her (him) the shield of faith, and clothe her (him) with Jesus himself.

Allow the faith, hope, and trust of Jesus to live in and through her (him) today, and may the light of Jesus shine through her (his) life! Amen.

> John 8:44; Revelation 19:11; Romans 13:14.

## THURSDAY: Think Within the Helmet of Salvation

*Lord, today I bow before you in prayer for these family members:*

Date: _____ Names: _____

Date: _____ Names: _____

Date: _____ Names: _____

Date: _____ Names: _____

## Scriptures

*Lord, your Word teaches…*

> Stand firm then…Take the helmet of salvation (Ephesians 6:14,17).

> Do not be anxious about anything, but in every situation, by prayer and petition, with thanksgiving, present your requests to God. And the peace of God, which transcends all understanding, will guard your hearts and your minds in Christ Jesus (Philippians 4:6-7).

## Daily Prayer Opener

Lord,

> My husband (wife, child, parent, brother, sister), _____ (insert name), is not strong enough to fight the evil one.

> If he (she) tries to fight the devil with his (her) own strength, he (she) will fail completely.

> Instead, I ask you to strengthen him (her), Lord, with your mighty power.

> As he (she) understands the need for physical protection, help him (her) grasp his (her) need for spiritual protection.

> I ask you to put on him (her) the very character of Christ, because it's light that overcomes darkness.

I ask you to put on him (her) your full armor, O God, so he (she) can take his (her) stand against the devil's schemes. Amen.

> Luke 22:31-32; 2 Chronicles 20:12; 2 Chronicles 16:9; Ephesians 1:19; 1 Samuel 17:38; Psalm 3:3; Romans 13:14; John 1:5; Ephesians 6:11.

## Armor Prayer

Lord,

Today is Thursday, so help _____ (insert name) "think within the helmet of salvation."

People today are so independent and self-assured.

They even believe they will go to heaven when they die because they consider themselves to be "pretty good" people.

How surprised they will be on the day of judgment when they learn that heaven is a perfect place where nothing impure can enter.

What a shock that will be—and I don't want him (her) to be one of them.

I thank you for Jesus, whose name is the only name by which he (she) can be saved.

So Lord, I ask you today to put on him (her) the helmet of salvation, and clothe him (her) with Jesus himself.

Allow the saving grace of Jesus to live in and through him (her), and may the light of Jesus shine through his (her) life! Amen.

> Revelation 21:27; Acts 4:12; Romans 13:14.

## FRIDAY: Fight with the Sword of the Spirit

*Lord, today I bow before you in prayer for these family members:*

Date: _____ Names: _____

Date: _____ Names: _____

Date: _____ Names: _____

Date: _____ Names: _____

### Scriptures

*Lord, your Word teaches...*

> Stand firm then...Take the sword of the Spirit, which is the word of God (Ephesians 6:14,17).

> Therefore, since we are surrounded by such a great cloud of witnesses, let us throw off everything that hinders and the sin that so easily entangles. And let us run with perseverance the race marked out for us, fixing our eyes on Jesus, the pioneer and perfecter of faith. For the joy set before him he endured the cross, scorning its shame, and sat down at the right hand of the throne of God (Hebrews 12:1-2).

### Daily Prayer Opener

Lord,

My husband (wife, child, parent, brother, sister), _____ (insert name), is not strong enough to fight the evil one.

If he (she) tries to fight the devil with his (her) own strength, he (she) will fail completely.

Instead, I ask you to strengthen him (her), Lord, with your mighty power.

As he (she) understands the need for physical protection, help him (her) grasp his (her) need for spiritual protection.

I ask you to put on him (her) the very character of Christ, because it's light that overcomes darkness.

I ask you to put on him (her) your full armor, O God, so he (she) can take his (her) stand against the devil's schemes. Amen.

> Luke 22:31-32; 2 Chronicles 20:12; 2 Chronicles 16:9; Ephesians 1:19; 1 Samuel 17:38; Psalm 3:3; Romans 13:14; John 1:5; Ephesians 6:11.

## Armor Prayer

Lord,

Today is Friday, so help _____ (insert name) "fight with the sword of the Spirit."

This world is filled with lots of opinions and theories, and people are so convinced their own way is best that they think they can even redefine words and morals.

Lord, I don't want her (him) to be one of them.

I want your Word to guide her (his) path, fill her (his) mind, comfort her (his) heart, and flow from her (his) lips.

I want her (him) to be like Jesus, who is the Word of God, and who defeated the enemy with Scripture.

So Lord, I ask you to arm her (him) with the sword of the Spirit, which is to clothe her (him) with Jesus himself.

Allow the Word of God to live in and through her (him) today, and may the light of Jesus shine through her (his) life! Amen.

> John 1:1; Romans 13:14.

## SATURDAY: Steadfastly Pray in the Spirit

*Lord, today I bow before you in prayer for these family members:*

Date: _____ Names: _____

Date: _____ Names: _____

Date: _____ Names: _____

Date: _____ Names: _____

### Scriptures

*Lord, your Word teaches…*

> Stand firm then…And pray in the Spirit on all occasions with all kinds of prayers and requests. With this in mind, be alert and always keep on praying for all the Lord's people (Ephesians 6:14,18).

> I will extol the LORD at all times;
>     his praise will always be on my lips.
>                         (Psalm 34:1)

### Daily Prayer Opener

Lord,

My husband (wife, child, parent, brother, sister), _____ (insert name), is not strong enough to fight the evil one.

If he (she) tries to fight the devil with his (her) own strength, he (she) will fail completely.

Instead, I ask you to strengthen him (her), Lord, with your mighty power.

As he (she) understands the need for physical protection, help him (her) grasp his (her) need for spiritual protection.

I ask you to put on him (her) the very character of Christ, because it's light that overcomes darkness.

I ask you to put on him (her) your full armor, O God, so he (she) can take his (her) stand against the devil's schemes. Amen.

> Luke 22:31-32; 2 Chronicles 20:12; 2 Chronicles 16:9; Ephesians 1:19; 1 Samuel 17:38; Psalm 3:3; Romans 13:14; John 1:5; Ephesians 6:11.

## Armor Prayer

Lord,

The week is now over, and on this Saturday I ask you to help _____ (insert name) "steadfastly pray in the Spirit."

This world is filled with people who doubt the power of prayer, and I don't want him (her) to be one of them.

I want him (her) to be like Jesus, who took time out of his busy schedule to pray, who taught his followers to pray, and who prayerfully sought his Father in his hour of need.

But every time he (she) tries to be like Jesus, I know that he (she) will fall short.

So Lord, I ask you today to fill him (her) with the prayerfulness of Jesus, and clothe him (her) with Jesus himself.

Allow Jesus to live in and through him (her) today, and give him (her) the desire to pray without ceasing.

May the light of Jesus shine through his (her) life! Amen.

> Mark 1:35; Luke 11:1-13; Luke 22:39-46; Romans 13:14.

# WEEK THREE

## Praying to Be Clothed with Christ

### Instructions for Week Three

This is a crucial week in learning to pray the armor of God, since to put on the armor is essentially to clothe ourselves with Christ. Because of this, this week's prayers are chock-full of Scripture. We can begin by writing the date and the names of those we would like to pray for, in addition to ourselves.

I suggest that we start with the prayer opener for ourselves, which for the first time is not written out in full because I hope we all have these memorized by now (refer back to page 72-73 if necessary). Then we will pray the day's prayer for ourselves.

After clothing ourselves with Christ in prayer, we can turn to clothing those we love in prayer. Begin with the prayer opener for others, and then pray the day's prayer again, this time for a specific family member or friend, inserting his or her name in the prayer and adjusting the pronouns and verbs as appropriate. Continue praying in this manner for as many people as time will allow. Let's give it a try.

### SUNDAY: Strap on the Belt of Truth

*Lord, I pray today for myself and for these people I love:*

Date: _____ Names: _____

(Use the following spaces for future weeks when you cycle again through these prayers.)

Date: _____ Names: _____

Date: _____ Names: _____

Date: _____ Names: _____

## Scriptures

*Lord, your Word teaches…*

> Stand firm then, with the belt of truth buckled around your waist (Ephesians 6:14).

> I saw heaven standing open and there before me a white horse, whose rider is called Faithful and True (Revelation 19:11).

## Daily Prayer Openers (for ourselves or others; see pages 72-73)

## Armor Prayer

Lord,

It's Sunday, so it's time to "strap on the belt of truth," which is nothing less than clothing ourselves in Christ, for you, Lord, are the way, the truth, and the life.

I ask you to strap on me (_____ [insert name]) the belt of truth.

Jesus, you are the holy and true God.

You are the true light that has come into the world.

You are the true bread that has come down from heaven.

You are the true vine, in whom we are to abide.

You are the true sanctuary, in whom we can now worship.

You alone are named Faithful and True.

So in asking for the belt of truth, I am asking for you;

I'm asking for your truth to reign in my (_____'s [insert name]) life, to fill me (him/her) and flow through my (his/her) life. Amen.

> Romans 13:14; John 14:6; Revelation 3:7; John 1:5; John 6:32;
> John 15:1; Hebrews 8:2; Revelation 19:11; Ephesians 4:21-24;
> John 7:38.

## MONDAY: Make Fast the Breastplate of Righteousness

*Lord, I pray today for myself and for these people I love:*

Date: _____ Names: _____

Date: _____ Names: _____

Date: _____ Names: _____

Date: _____ Names: _____

## Scriptures

*Lord, your Word teaches…*

> Stand firm then…with the breastplate of righteousness in place (Ephesians 6:14).

> "God…has chosen you to know his will and to see the Righteous One" (Acts 22:14).

## Daily Prayer Openers (for ourselves or others; see pages 72-73)

## Armor Prayer

Lord,

On Monday I take these moments to "make fast the breastplate of righteousness," which is to put on Christ.

I ask you to make fast the breastplate of righteousness on me

(_____ [insert name]), for Jesus is the very righteousness of God in human form.

Jesus, the only one who knew no sin, became sin on my (her/his) behalf, to make me (her/him) perfect forever, fit for a perfect heaven.

Because of my (her/his) sin, Jesus was led like a lamb to the slaughter and became the spotless lamb who took away my (her/his) sin.

I ask that Jesus would be a shield about me (_____ [insert name]), and grant me (her/him) the righteousness that comes by faith in Christ.

I pray that Jesus' righteousness might reign in my (her/his) life; may I (she/he) always seek first his kingdom and righteousness. Amen.

> Romans 13:14; 1 Corinthians 1:30; 2 Corinthians 5:21;
> Hebrews 10:14; Isaiah 53:7; 1 Corinthians 5:7; Psalm 28:7;
> Romans 3:22; Romans 3:21-26; Matthew 6:33.

## TUESDAY: Tread in the Shoes of Peace

*Lord, I pray today for myself and for these people I love:*

Date: _____ Names: _____

Date: _____ Names: _____

Date: _____ Names: _____

Date: _____ Names: _____

## Scriptures

*Lord, your Word teaches…*

> Stand firm then…with your feet fitted with the readiness that comes from the gospel of peace (Ephesians 6:14-15).

> For he himself is our peace (Ephesians 2:14).

## Daily Prayer Openers (for ourselves or others; see pages 72-73)

## Armor Prayer

Lord,

Today is Tuesday, so I ask you to empower us to "tread in the shoes of peace," which is to put on Christ, because he himself is our peace.

I ask you to help me (_____ [insert name]), to walk in the shoes of peace, which is to walk in the ways of Jesus, the Prince of Peace himself.

Jesus is the Lord and creator of peace, the only one who is able to give me (him/her) peace at all times and in every way.

He is the one who can keep me (him/her) in perfect peace, as my (his/her) mind is steadfast, trusting in you, O Lord.

May the peace of Christ rule in my (his/her) heart, and may the peace that passes understanding guard my (_____ [insert name])'s heart and mind in Christ Jesus.

Thank you that in and through the Lord Jesus Christ, I (he/she) have (has) peace with God and I (he/she) can rejoice in hope. Amen.

> Ephesians 2:14; Isaiah 9:6; 2 Thessalonians 3:16; Isaiah 26:3; Psalm 22:5; Colossians 3:15; Romans 5:1; Philippians 4:7; Romans 5:1-2.

## WEDNESDAY: Wield the Shield of Faith

*Lord, I pray today for myself and for these people I love:*

Date: _____ Names: _____

Date: _____ Names: _____

Date: _____ Names: _____

Date: _____ Names: _____

## Scriptures

*Lord, your Word teaches…*

> Stand firm then…[and] take up the shield of faith, with which you can extinguish all the flaming arrows of the evil one (Ephesians 6:14,16).

> I saw heaven standing open and there before me was a white horse, whose rider is called Faithful and True…He is dressed in a robe dipped in blood, and his name is the Word of God (Revelation 19:11,13).

## Daily Prayer Openers (for ourselves or others; see pages 72-73)

## Armor Prayer

Lord,

> It's Wednesday, so I ask you to help me (_____ [insert name]) "wield the shield of faith," which is the same as to ask you, O God, to clothe me (_____) with Christ, who is called Faithful and True.

> I pray that Christ be the author and perfecter of my (his/her) faith, who for the joy set before him endured the cross.

> Christ was faithful as a son, so I (he/she) can be adopted because of Jesus into your family.

I pray that I (_____) may live by faith in the Son of God, who loved me (him/her) and gave himself up for me (him/her).

I pray this in the faithful name of Jesus, for he alone is both holy and true. Amen.

Revelation 19:11; Hebrews 12:2; Hebrews 3:6; Ephesians 1:5; Galatians 2:20; Revelation 3:7.

## THURSDAY: Think Within the Helmet of Salvation

*Lord, I pray today for myself and for these people I love:*

Date: _____ Names: _____

Date: _____ Names: _____

Date: _____ Names: _____

Date: _____ Names: _____

## Scriptures

*Lord, your Word teaches…*

Stand firm then…Take the helmet of salvation (Ephesians 6:14,17).

"Today…a Savior has been born to you; he is the Messiah, the Lord" (Luke 2:11).

## Daily Prayer Openers (for ourselves or others; see pages 72-73)

## Armor Prayer

Lord,

It's Thursday, so I ask you to help me (_____ [insert name]) "think within the helmet of salvation," which is to have the mind of Christ, because Jesus is salvation.

Isaiah said, "Say to Daughter Zion, 'See, your Savior comes!'"

Jeremiah prophesied, "This is the name by which he will be called: The LORD Our Righteous Savior."

Micah, after predicting the Savior would be born in tiny Bethlehem, said, "I watch in hope for the LORD, I wait for God my Savior."

The Samaritan villagers said, "We know that this man really is the Savior of the world."

Titus preached, "We wait for the blessed hope—the appearing of the glory of our great God and Savior, Jesus Christ."

This Savior is none other than Jesus, God come to earth to save us.

Allow my (_____)'s thoughts to be occupied with Jesus today. Amen.

> Isaiah 62:11; Jeremiah 23:6; Micah 5:2; 7:7; John 4:42; Titus 2:13; John 1:14.

## FRIDAY: Fight with the Sword of the Spirit

*Lord, I pray today for myself and for these people I love:*

Date: _____ Names: _____

Date: _____ Names: _____

Date: _____ Names: _____

Date: _____ Names: _____

## Scriptures

*Lord, your Word teaches...*

> Stand firm then...Take the sword of the Spirit, which is the word of God (Ephesians 6:14,17).

In the beginning was the Word, and the Word was with God, and the Word was God…The Word became flesh and made his dwelling among us (John 1:1,14).

## Daily Prayer Openers (for ourselves or others; see pages 72-73)

## Armor Prayer

Lord,

Today is Friday, so I ask you to help me (_____ [insert name]) "fight with the sword of the Spirit."

Help me (her/him) remember that the sword is a who, not a what, for the sword is the Word of God, who is Jesus himself.

Jesus is no mere prophet, teacher, miracle-worker or revolutionary; he is God! [Let that sink in for a moment.]

Teach me (her/him) to see Jesus as the book of Revelation describes, "He is dressed in a robe dipped in blood, and his name is the Word of God."

May the Word of God live in me (her/him), may the Word of God spread and flourish through me (her/him), and may I (she/he) forever be sustained by the powerful Word. Amen.

> John 1:1,14; John 20:28; Titus 2:13; Revelation 19:13; 1 John 2:14; Acts 12:24; Hebrews 1:3.

## SATURDAY: Steadfastly Pray in the Spirit

*Lord, I pray today for myself and for these people I love:*

Date: _____ Names: _____

Date: _____ Names: _____

Date: _____ Names: _____

Date: _____ Names: _____

## Scriptures

*Lord, your Word teaches...*

> Stand firm then...And pray in the Spirit on all occasions
> with all kinds of prayers and requests. With this in mind,
> be alert and always keep on praying for all the Lord's people
> (Ephesians 6:14,18).

> God sent the Spirit of his Son into our hearts (Galatians
> 4:6).

## Daily Prayer Openers (for ourselves or others; see pages 72-73)

## Armor Prayer

Lord,

It's the end of the week again, so I want to take a few moments
and thank you for the blessings and challenges of this week,
and I ask you to help me (_____ [insert name]) "steadfastly pray in the Spirit."

Help me (him/her) to grow in my (his/her) understanding of the
Trinity, also known as the Three-in-One and as the Godhead.

Help me (him/her) always be aware that a full understanding of
you is beyond my (his/her) grasp in this life, for while on earth
we (he/she) only see(s) dimly and knows in part.

Allow me (him/her) to become better acquainted with each person in the Godhead, and to understand that the Spirit is not some mystical force, but is forever united and described as the Spirit of Christ, and is even called the Spirit of Jesus.

In the name of the Father and of the Son and of the Holy Spirit. Amen.

Colossians 2:9; 1 Corinthians 13:12; Romans 8:9; Acts 16:7.

# WEEK FOUR

## Praying for Spouses and Marriages

### Instructions for Week Four

As we move ahead in our prayer journey, the focus this week is on spouses and marriages. I am aware that some singles might be uncomfortable with this prayer emphasis, so they may prefer to skip ahead to Week Five: "Praying for Friends and Single Adults." Other singles will be very happy to pray these prayers for spouses and marriages, since many of their loved ones are married—possibly even struggling in their marriages and in deep need of prayer. In many cases, if we don't pray for them, who will?

So if you are single, just substitute the names of your married friends or family members in place of "my marriage" or "my spouse." If you are married, first pray each day this week for your own marriage, and then pray for others' marriages.

### SUNDAY: Strap on the Belt of Truth

*Lord, I humbly bow before you today and pray for these marriages:*

Date: _____ Names: _____

(Use the following spaces for future weeks when you cycle again through these prayers.)

Date: _____ Names: _____

Date: _____ Names: _____

Date: _____ Names: _____

## Scriptures

*Lord, your Word teaches...*

> Stand firm then, with the belt of truth buckled around your waist (Ephesians 6:14).

> "Sanctify them by the truth; your word is truth" (John 17:17).

## Daily Prayer Openers (for ourselves or others; see pages 72-73)

## Armor Prayer

Lord,

It's Sunday, so I pray that you would "strap the belt of truth" around my marriage (around _____ and _____'s marriage), and that you would allow my spouse, _____, and me (them) to walk in your truth all the days of our (their) lives.

I pray that you would sanctify our (their) marriage by your Word; help us (them) pattern our (their) marriage according to your ways.

Inspire us (them) to lay down our (their) lives for each other as you did for your bride, the church.

I pray that you, Jesus, the Light of the world, would completely illuminate our (their) marriage with your truth.

I pray that we (they) would see each other as you see us (them), as beloved, cleansed, and forgiven.

I pray that your truth would shine in every corner of our (their) minds, hearts, bodies, and souls.

I pray the light of your glory would drive out any darkness, any deception, any divisiveness from our (their) lives.

I pray that the light of your purity would heal any disease or distress or impurity.

Please let us (them) walk in your love all the days of our (their) lives, and then dwell together with you in heaven above—forever. Amen.

> 3 John 3; John 17:17; Psalm 119:1; John 15:13; Ephesians 5:25; John 8:12; Ephesians 5:13; 1 Corinthians 13:12; Hebrews 9:22; Psalm 67:1; Mark 12:30; 1 Peter 2:9; 2 Corinthians 4:2; 1 John 1:7; Luke 8:50; Psalm 90:14; Psalm 23:6.

## MONDAY: Make Fast the Breastplate of Righteousness

*Lord, I humbly bow before you today and pray for these marriages:*

Date: _____ Names: _____

Date: _____ Names: _____

Date: _____ Names: _____

Date: _____ Names: _____

## Scriptures

*Lord, your Word teaches…*

> Stand firm then…with the breastplate of righteousness in place (Ephesians 6:14).

> May God himself, the God of peace, sanctify you through and through. May your whole spirit, soul and body be kept

blameless at the coming of our Lord Jesus Christ (1 Thessalonians 5:23).

## Daily Prayer Openers (for ourselves or others; see pages 72-73)

## Armor Prayer

Lord,

I pray on this Monday that you would "make fast the breastplate of righteousness" on our marriage (on the marriage of _____ and _____).

I pray for my spouse, _____ (for _____ and _____), that you would sanctify her/him (them) through and through.

May our (their) marriage bed remain pure, and may our (their) hearts and minds remain unsoiled by this world.

I pray you would help us (them) keep our (their) minds holy, and enable us (them) to think only about whatever things are true, noble, right, pure, lovely, admirable, excellent, and praiseworthy.

Please help us (them) be righteous examples to our (their) children, and set a pattern worthy for them to follow.

I pray that you would give us (them) the wisdom and strength to keep from being polluted by this world.

And may a thousand generations that follow us (them) praise your name and be filled with your love. Amen.

> 1 Thessalonians 5:23; Hebrews 13:4; Revelation 3:4; 1 Peter
> 1:13-15; Philippians 4:8; Ephesians 5:1; 2 Timothy 1:13; James
> 1:27; Exodus 20:6.

## TUESDAY: Tread in the Shoes of Peace

*Lord, I humbly bow before you today and pray for these marriages:*

Date: _____ Names: _____

Date: _____ Names: _____

Date: _____ Names: _____

Date: _____ Names: _____

## Scriptures

*Lord, your Word teaches…*

> Stand firm then…with your feet fitted with the readiness that comes from the gospel of peace (Ephesians 6:14-15).

> If it is possible, as far as it depends on you, live at peace with everyone (Romans 12:18).

## Daily Prayer Openers (for ourselves or others; see pages 72-73)

## Armor Prayer

Lord,

I pray for my spouse, _____ (for the marriage of _____ and _____), that you would put on him/her (them) "the shoes of peace."

Fill him/her (them) today, Father, Son, and Holy Spirit, fill him/her (them) with the unity of the Trinity, fill him/her (them) with the very love you have shared within yourself, O God, from eternity.

When difficult people (especially me!) bring conflict into his/her (their) life (lives), help him/her (them) to be the peacemaker(s).

When differences and disagreements arise, guide him/her (them) to know what are essentials, what are nonessentials, and how he/she (they) can always act in love.

In this world where friendships and families seldom last, where divorce, betrayals, and even wars abound, give him/her (them) the jungle boots of peace, strong enough to endure the battles the foe will throw at him/her (them).

And especially help him/her (them) know, in the deepest parts of his/her (their) heart(s) and soul(s), that because of Jesus Christ he/she (they) is (are) at peace with you, O God, now and forevermore.

And that one day he/she (they) and his/her (their) loved ones in Christ, will be reunited in glory and serenity for eternity. Amen.

> Isaiah 52:7; Matthew 28:19; Colossian 2:9; John 17:23-24; John 16:33; James 3:18; Acts 15:2; 1 Corinthians 15:1-4; Acts 15:28; 1 Corinthians 13:1-3; Acts 15:39; Mark 13:7; Nahum 1:15; 1 Corinthians 10:13; Matthew 13:39; Philippians 3:8; Ephesians 1:18; 1 Corinthians 1:4; Romans 5:1; Psalm 121:8; Romans 16:8; 1 Thessalonians 4:17.

## WEDNESDAY: Wield the Shield of Faith

*Lord, I humbly bow before you today and pray for these marriages:*

Date: _____ Names: _____

Date: _____ Names: _____

Date: _____ Names: _____

Date: _____ Names: _____

## Scriptures

*Lord, your Word teaches…*

> Stand firm then…[and] take up the shield of faith, with which you can extinguish all the flaming arrows of the evil one (Ephesians 6:14,16).

By faith Noah, when warned about things not yet seen, in holy fear built an ark to save his family. By his faith he condemned the world and became heir of the righteousness that is in keeping with faith (Hebrews 11:7).

## Daily Prayer Openers (for ourselves or others; see pages 72-73)

## Armor Prayer

Lord,

It's Wednesday, and we desire to "wield the shield of faith" in our marriage (in the marriage of _____ and _____).

I pray for my spouse, _____, and our marriage (for _____ and _____ and their marriage) that our (their) faith would not rest on human wisdom, but on your power.

Please put on us (them) the faith of Noah, who in holy faith built the ark and saved his family—and all humanity—from destruction.

I ask you to put on us (them) the faith of Abraham, who believed in you and was credited with righteousness.

In our (their) marriage may we (they) choose to trust you with all our (their) hearts, and not lean on our (their) own understanding.

In all our (their) ways may we (they) submit to you, for we know you promise to make our (their) paths straight.

As spouses, help us (them) not to be wise in our (their) own eyes; but help us (them) to fear you, O Lord, and shun evil.

This will bring health to our (their) marriage, for we (they) are one body, and it will bring nourishment to our (their) souls. Amen.

1 Corinthians 2:5; Hebrews 11:7; Romans 4:3; Proverbs 3:5; Proverbs 3:6; Proverbs 3:7; Genesis 2:24; Proverbs 3:8.

## THURSDAY: Think Within the Helmet of Salvation

*Lord, I humbly bow before you today and pray for these marriages:*

Date: _____ Names: _____

Date: _____ Names: _____

Date: _____ Names: _____

Date: _____ Names: _____

## Scriptures

*Lord, your Word teaches…*

> Stand firm then…Take the helmet of salvation (Ephesians 6:14,17).

> You will keep in perfect peace
>     those whose minds are steadfast,
>     because they trust in you.
>                               (Isaiah 26:3)

## Daily Prayer Openers (for ourselves or others; see pages 72-73)

## Armor Prayer

Lord,

In this world our minds are a mess and our thoughts are darkened, and we are filled with worries, fears, and anxious thoughts.

I ask on this Thursday that you help us "think within the helmet of salvation," and teach us in our marriage (teach _____ and _____ in their marriage) to set our (their) minds on things above.

Please come into our (their) lives and take control of our (their) minds; cleanse our (their) consciences so we (they) can better serve you.

I pray our (their) marriage could be like a tree planted by the water, sending its roots to the stream.

Then we (they) will not fear when heat comes, our (their) leaves will always be green; we (they) will have no worries in a year of drought, and never fail to bear fruit.

Help us (them) take every thought captive and make it obedient to Christ.

Help us (them) not to say everything that crosses our (their) minds, but to be quick to listen, slow to speak, and slow to become angry.

Please help our (their) marriage to not be conformed to this world, but transformed by the renewing of our (their) minds.

Then we (they) will be able to test and approve what your will is, and we (they) will not think more highly of ourselves (themselves) than we (they) should. Amen.

> Romans 1:21; Mark 4:19; Colossians 3:2; Proverbs 32:9; Hebrews 9:14; Psalm 1:3; Jeremiah 17:8; 2 Corinthians 10:5; James 1:19; Romans 12:1-2; Romans 12:3.

## FRIDAY: Fight with the Sword of the Spirit

*Lord, I humbly bow before you today and pray for these marriages:*

Date: _____ Names: _____

Date: _____ Names: _____

Date: _____ Names: _____

Date: _____ Names: _____

## Scriptures

*Lord, your Word teaches…*

> Stand firm then…Take the sword of the Spirit, which is the Word of God (Ephesians 6:14,17).

> Husbands, love your wives, just as Christ loved the church and gave himself up for her to make her holy, cleansing her by the washing with water through the word, and to present her to himself as a radiant church, without stain or wrinkle or any other blemish, but holy and blameless (Ephesians 5:25-27).

## Daily Prayer Openers (for ourselves or others; see pages 72-73)

## Armor Prayer

Lord,

My spouse and I desire your Word to be the foundation of our (_____ and _____'s) marriage, so this Friday I ask you to help us (them) "fight with the sword of the Spirit."

Help us (them) to love each other as Christ loved the church, washing and cleansing our (their) marriage by the purity of your Word.

We desire (Give them the desire) to build our (their) marriage on your words, which means that we (they) will build our (their) house on the rock.

When the rains fall, streams rise, and winds blow, our (their) marriage will be secure and will not fall.

Help us (them) to be not merely hearers of your Word but doers, for those that do not put your words into practice have built their family on sandy ground and such a house will fall with a great crash.

May we (they) know that the fear of the Lord is the beginning of knowledge, and that you, O Lord, give wisdom and understanding.

May our (their) marriage be filled with your Word, wisdom, and truth. Amen.

> Ephesians 5:25; Ephesians 5:26; Matthew 7:24; Matthew 7:25; James 1:25; Matthew 7:26-27; Proverbs 1:7; Proverbs 2:6.

## SATURDAY: Steadfastly Pray in the Spirit

*Lord, I humbly bow before you today and pray for these marriages:*

Date: _____ Names: _____

Date: _____ Names: _____

Date: _____ Names: _____

Date: _____ Names: _____

## Scriptures

*Lord, your Word teaches…*

> Stand firm then…And pray in the Spirit on all occasions with all kinds of prayers and requests. With this in mind, be alert and always keep on praying for all the Lord's people (Ephesians 6:14,18).

> Husbands…be considerate as you live with your wives, and treat them with respect…so that nothing will hinder your prayers (1 Peter 3:7).

> "For this reason a man will leave his father and mother and be united to his wife, and the two will become one flesh." This is a profound mystery—but I am talking about Christ and the church. However, each one of you also must love

his wife as he loves himself, and the wife must respect her husband (Ephesians 5:31-33).

## Daily Prayer Openers (for ourselves or others; see pages 72-73)

## Armor Prayer

Lord,

On this Saturday I "steadfastly pray in the Spirit" for our marriage (the marriage of _____ and _____).

We (they) have left fathers and mothers behind, and have become united in the bonds of matrimony.

We (they) were once two persons, separate and self-directed, but now we (they) are one flesh, united in body, soul, and spirit.

We (they) are participants in this divine mystery, which is a living picture of Christ and the church.

As Christ loved the church and gave himself up for her, please help us (them) love each other with true Christlike love, sacrificing and giving ourselves (themselves) up for one another.

Please help us (them) love each other as we (they) love ourselves (themselves), and help us (them) show respect to one another, so our (their) prayers will not be hindered.

May our (their) marriage be a living example of your power, able to make two broken people into one redeemed whole. Amen.

> Ephesians 5:31; Ephesians 5:31; Ephesians 5:32; Ephesians 5:25; Ephesians 5:33; 1 Peter 3:7; Psalm 107:2.

# WEEK FIVE

## Praying for Friends and Single Adults

### Instructions for Week Five

Single adults often get the short end of the stick in churches today. With the exception of the Catholic church, married people lead most churches. This means that the majority of sermons are taught from a marital perspective, married leaders frequently design children and student programs, and even women's and men's ministries are usually led by married folk.

This is exceptionally strange when we remember that Jesus himself was single, as was the apostle Paul. It is also strategically flawed because over 40 percent of the adults in America are unmarried. I believe there are more unchurched single households in most cities today than married folks who don't attend church. In other words, most of the people churches are trying to reach are unmarried.

So it is vital that we pray for singles, both inside and outside the church. At the same time, we can pray for friends who are not a part of our immediate or extended family. And this week we will try something new: we will target different groups of friends and singles each day of the week. This gives us yet another way of praying the armor of God. (By the way, these topics can also be adapted for ourselves or our married friends. As you pray, if something reminds you of others who need the same prayer, jot their names on the side and pray for them also, regardless of marital status.)

## SUNDAY: Strap on the Belt of Truth

*Lord, today I want to pray for these singles who are my friends:*

Date: _____ Names: _____

(Use the following spaces for future weeks when you cycle again through these prayers.)

Date: _____ Names: _____

Date: _____ Names: _____

Date: _____ Names: _____

## Scriptures

*Lord, your Word teaches…*

> Stand firm then, with the belt of truth buckled around your waist (Ephesians 6:14).

> Behold, You desire truth in the innermost being,
> And in the hidden part You will make me know wisdom.
> (Psalm 51:6 NASB)

## Daily Prayer Openers (for ourselves or others; see pages 72-73)

## Armor Prayer

Lord,

It's Sunday, so it's a great opportunity to "strap on the belt of truth."

I pray for my unmarried friend _____ (insert name), that you, O Lord, would increase her (his) understanding of your truth, and fill her (him) with truth in her (his) inner being.

I pray that she (he) may always desire to be a person of honesty; that she (he) may hunger for your truth, and that you would strengthen her (him) with your truth.

I pray for her (his) church to be a beacon of truth, for in this world, side by side, we fight the good fight of truth.

I pray that the eyes of her (his) heart might be enlightened so that she (he) may grasp how wide, long, high, and deep is the love of Christ, and experience your love that surpasses knowledge, and be filled to the measure of all the fullness of God.

I pray this in the Faithful and True name of Jesus. Amen.

> Proverbs 23:23; Psalm 51:6; Proverbs 12:17; Deuteronomy 8:3; Psalm 119:28; Matthew 5:14-15; Colossians 2:1; Ephesians 1:18; Ephesians 3:18; Ephesians 3:19; Revelation 19:11.

## MONDAY: Make Fast the Breastplate of Righteousness

*Lord, today I want to pray for singles/friends who may be struggling with temptation:*

Date: _____ Names: _____

Date: _____ Names: _____

Date: _____ Names: _____

Date: _____ Names: _____

## Scriptures

*Lord, your Word teaches...*

Stand firm then...with the breastplate of righteousness in place (Ephesians 6:14).

Let love and faithfulness never leave you;
    bind them around your neck,
    write them on the tablet of your heart.
                    (Proverbs 3:3)

## Daily Prayer Openers (for ourselves or others; see pages 72-73)

## Armor Prayer

Lord,

I pray on this Monday that you "make fast the breastplate of righteousness" to protect the heart of _____.

This world is an ethically dangerous place, and many people think it's their right to redefine morality.

Today the whole world seems to be confused and misguided; up is called down and wrong is said to be right.

So I pray that integrity and uprightness will protect my friend.

I pray that you put on him (her) the breastplate of righteousness; write faithfulness and love on the tablets of his (her) heart.

I pray that you also put on him (her) your breastplate of faith and love.

I pray that you lead him (her) not into temptation, but deliver him (her) from the evil one.

Give _____ the wisdom to discern when he (she) is being tempted, and the strength and endurance to withstand evil enticements.

Please guide him (her) today in the paths of righteousness, for that is the way of life, and along that path is life eternal.

I pray this in the name of the King of Righteousness. Amen.

> Acts 19:29; Psalm 25:21; Isaiah 59:17; Proverbs 3:3; 1 Thessalonians 5:8; Matthew 6:13; James 1:14; Proverbs 8:20; Proverbs 12:28.

## TUESDAY: Tread in the Shoes of Peace

*Lord, today I want to pray for friends who are divorced or struggling in relationships:*

Date: _____ Names: _____

Date: _____ Names: _____

Date: _____ Names: _____

Date: _____ Names: _____

### Scriptures

*Lord, your Word teaches…*

> Stand firm then…with your feet fitted with the readiness
> that comes from the gospel of peace (Ephesians 6:14-15).

> In peace I will lie down and sleep,
>     for you alone, LORD,
>     make me dwell in safety.
>                         (Psalm 4:8)

### Daily Prayer Openers (for ourselves or others; see pages 72-73)

### Armor Prayer

Lord,

I pray on this Tuesday that you help my friend _____ "tread
in the shoes of peace."

I pray that your peace would be a firm foundation for her (his)
life, and that you fill her (him) with all joy and peace as she (he)
trusts in you.

Lord, _____'s life has not been easy, and the evil one has
caused some of her (his) relationships to fail.

She (he) probably feels guilty about her (his) broken marriage (or friendship) and carries around a weight of self-condemnation and unforgiveness.

I pray that you would remind her (him) that even your spouse, Israel, was unfaithful; you hate divorce because you, O God, have been through it.

Help her (him) not to consider herself (himself) a second-class Christian because she (he) has been divorced, for that would imply that you are a second-class God.

I pray that she (he) would know that once we confess our sin we are forgiven and washed as white as snow.

From this day forward, please inspire her (him) to be a peacemaker and conflict-resolver in this world so infected by discord and division.

I pray that you help _____, as far as it is possible, to be at peace with all people.

Please keep us in your perfect peace, for we trust in you, as I pray this in the name of the Prince of Peace. Amen.

2 Timothy 2:19; Romans 15:13; Malachi 2:16; Jeremiah 3:8; 1 John 1:9; Psalm 51:7; James 3:18; 1 Corinthians 1:10; Romans 12:18; Isaiah 26:3; Isaiah 9:6.

## WEDNESDAY: Wield the Shield of Faith

*Lord, today I want to pray for friends who may be struggling with doubt:*

Date: _____ Names: _____

Date: _____ Names: _____

Date: _____ Names: _____

Date: _____ Names: _____

## Scriptures

*Lord, your Word teaches...*

> Stand firm then...[and] take up the shield of faith, with which you can extinguish all the flaming arrows of the evil one (Ephesians 6:14,16).

> When I am afraid, I put my trust in you.
>> In God, whose word I praise—
> in God I trust and am not afraid.
>> What can mere mortals do to me?
>>> (Psalm 56:3-4)

## Daily Prayer Openers (for ourselves or others; see pages 72-73)

### Armor Prayer

Lord,

It's Wednesday, so I ask you to help us "wield the shield of faith," and I especially pray that you put this shield around _____.

As the apostles asked Jesus, "Increase our faith!," so I ask you to increase his (her) faith and decrease his (her) doubts.

Help him (her) believe, and help him (her) overcome his (her) unbelief.

I pray that _____ will walk by faith, not sight.

I pray that you would strengthen him (her) in the faith, and convince him (her) of the need to be an active part of a church, where we fight, side by side, the good fight of faith against evil.

When doubts assail him (her), and questions and uncertainties darken his (her) mind, may you provide just enough light to keep his (her) faith strong and alive, but also the humility to know that he (she) will never have all the answers on this side of glory.

Above all, I pray that _____ finds saving faith in Jesus and
that he (she) would walk with you all the days of his (her) life.

I pray this in the Faithful and True name of Jesus. Amen.

Luke 17:5; Mark 9:24; 2 Corinthians 5:7; Colossians 2:7;
1 Timothy 6:12; 1 Corinthians 13:12; Romans 1:8; 3 John 4.

## THURSDAY: Think Within the Helmet of Salvation

*Lord, today I want to pray for friends who may be atheists or agnostics:*

Date: _____ Names: _____

Date: _____ Names: _____

Date: _____ Names: _____

Date: _____ Names: _____

## Scriptures

*Lord, your Word teaches…*

Stand firm then…Take the helmet of salvation (Ephesians
6:14,17).

The LORD is my rock, my fortress and my deliverer;
my God is my rock, in whom I take refuge,
my shield and the horn of my salvation, my stronghold.
(Psalm 18:2)

## Daily Prayer Openers (for ourselves or others; see pages 72-73)

### Armor Prayer

Lord,

Today is Thursday, so help me "think within the helmet of salvation."

I also pray that you would put the helmet of salvation on

_____.

It seems like secularism and skepticism are winning in our world today, that these worldviews have taken over media, schools, and government, and there are more and more voices that say there is no God.

But your Word bluntly says, "The fool says in his heart, 'There is no God.'"

So I pray that _____ would discover that you not only exist, but you are a loving, wise, and forgiving God who has revealed yourself in Jesus Christ.

I pray that she (he) would realize this and become a Christian.

I pray that she (he) would deeply grasp that all knowledge is based on faith, that those who dismiss faith in God or the Bible ultimately have faith only in themselves, which is surely an inadequate, imperfect, and misplaced faith.

I pray that you would open the eyes of her (his) heart, so that she (he) would grasp that Christianity is actually true.

I pray that she (he) would overflow with thankfulness for your saving love, knowing that salvation was purchased at the high cost of the cross.

Help her (him) know there is no way she (he) could ever earn salvation; that salvation is by far the greatest gift she (he) will ever be given.

Though she (he) is now far from you, I pray for her (him) to hear your summoning grace and come to saving faith.

Finally, I pray not only for my friend's salvation, but I pray for
everyone in the world and for peoples of all nations to be saved.

I pray this in the name of the one and only Savior, Jesus. Amen.

> Psalm 14:1; Acts 26:28; Ephesians 1:18; Colossians 2:7; Colossians 2:13-15; Titus 3:4-5; Romans 6:23; John 4:42; Luke 19:9; 1 Timothy 2:4; Acts 4:12.

## FRIDAY: Fight with the Sword of the Spirit

*Lord, today I will pray for my friends to be equipped with and hunger for your Word:*

Date: _____ Names: _____

Date: _____ Names: _____

Date: _____ Names: _____

Date: _____ Names: _____

## Scriptures
*Lord, your Word teaches…*

> Stand firm then…Take the sword of the Spirit, which is
> the word of God (Ephesians 6:14,17).

> As for God, his way is perfect:
> The Lord's word is flawless;
> he shields all who take refuge in him.
> (Psalm 18:30)

## Daily Prayer Openers (for ourselves or others; see pages 72-73)

## Armor Prayer

Lord,

Today is Friday, so help me "fight with the sword of the Spirit."

I pray also for my friend _____ that you would help him (her) fight with the sword of the Spirit.

I am so thankful for your Word, which is a mighty weapon and also a source of peace and comfort.

Help _____ to become very familiar with your Word; put your precepts in both his (her) mind and his (her) heart.

I pray that he (she) would hunger and thirst for your Word, and to grow to trust your Word more than he (she) trusts himself (herself).

I pray that he (she) will follow your Word and that it would be a lamp to his (her) feet and a light to his (her) path.

I pray also for the church _____ is a part of, that it would faithfully teach and live out the Word.

I pray not just for my friend, but I also ask that the leaders in our nation would return to your Word, for without your counsel no nation can prosper or survive.

I pray this in the name of the living Word, Jesus. Amen.

> Hebrews 4:12; Psalm 119:52; Psalm 139:3; Job 22:22; Psalm 119:66; Psalm 119:63; Psalm 119:105; Hebrews 5:12; Psalm 2:1; Revelation 1:18.

## SATURDAY: Steadfastly Pray in the Spirit

*Lord, today I will pray for singles or others who may be struggling with discontentment:*

Date: _____ Names: _____

Date: _____ Names: _____

Date: _____ Names: _____

Date: _____ Names: _____

### Scriptures

*Lord, your Word teaches…*

> Stand firm then…And pray in the Spirit on all occasions with all kinds of prayers and requests. With this in mind, be alert and always keep on praying for all the Lord's people (Ephesians 6:14,18).

> Praise the Lord [*Hallelu Yah*].
> Praise the Lord, my soul.
> I will praise the Lord all my life;
>     I will sing praise to my God as long as I live.
>                     (Psalm 146:1-2)

### Daily Prayer Openers (for ourselves or others; see pages 72-73)

### Armor Prayer

Lord,

The week is now over, and on this Saturday I ask you to help me steadfastly pray in the Spirit.

I also ask that you help _____ steadfastly pray in the Spirit because she (he) seems to be struggling with discontentment.

Help her (him) to learn to rest in you and to find her (his) satisfaction in you.

Help her (him) learn to pray in the Spirit on all occasions, with all kinds of prayers and requests.

Help her (him) learn to pray without ceasing, and give her (him) a love for prayer.

This world is so full of empty promises and so many discouraged and disillusioned people.

I pray that you would encourage _____ in her (his) spirit, and give her (him) a strong church where people encourage one another.

Help her (him) to learn the secret of being content in any and every situation, and that she (he) can do everything through Christ who gives us strength.

Help her (him) to experience the peace that passes understanding and enter your rest, O Lord, which has come to us in Christ. Amen.

> Romans 12:12; Philippians 4:6; 1 Thessalonians 5:17; Psalm 42:8; Hebrews 10:25; Philippians 4:12-13; Philippians 4:7; Hebrews 4:3.

# WEEK SIX

# Praying for Children and Teenagers

### Instructions for Week Six

In the Bible, Abraham prayed for the king of Gerar to have children (Genesis 20:17), Isaac prayed for the safety of his children (Genesis 32:11), Hannah prayed to become pregnant (1 Samuel 1:11), and Eli prayed for Elkanah and Hannah to have more children (1 Samuel 2:20). Most famously, people brought their children to Jesus and asked him to lay his hands on them and pray for them (Matthew 19:13). Praying for children is very biblical.

As the father of three children, this is perhaps my favorite topic to pray in this ten-week series. I love praying the armor of God for my kids in the morning and evening, but I also pray for them several times a day because, as every parent knows, our kids are never far from our hearts. Reminders of them appear in my mind, unbidden, throughout the day. It may be the sight of someone else's child, the sound of kids on a playground, or even the glance of a car that is similar to the model driven by one of my kids. When I am reminded of one of my children, I often think, *I wonder what they are doing? What might they be dealing with right now? How can I pray for them?* I then ask myself, *Well, what day of the week is it?* If it's Sunday, I offer a quick prayer for God to "strap the belt of truth" on them, to help them be people of truth, and to enable them to see the truth about whatever situation they are dealing with at that moment.

If you do not have children of your own, I'll bet there are still children in your life whom you love, children on whom you can ask God to put his armor. Think of your extended family, friends, neighbors, and church families. You can make a difference in the lives of children—through prayer. (If this topic is, for personal reasons, too painful or difficult, feel free to skip to the next week in this prayer guide.)

Write today's date and the names of two or three kids, and pray the following prayers for each of them, one at a time (if you have more time—or more kids—feel free to add more names).

## SUNDAY: Strap on the Belt of Truth

*Lord, I come before you as your beloved child, and I pray for these children whom I love:*

Date: _____ Names: _____

(Use the following spaces for future weeks when you cycle again through these prayers.)

Date: _____ Names: _____

Date: _____ Names: _____

Date: _____ Names: _____

### Scriptures

*Lord, your Word teaches…*

> Stand firm then, with the belt of truth buckled around your waist (Ephesians 6:14).

> I have no greater joy than to hear that my children are walking in the truth (3 John 4).

### Daily Prayer Openers (for ourselves or others; see pages 72-73)

### Armor Prayer

Lord,

It's Sunday, so it's a reminder to "strap the belt of truth" on those I love.

I pray for a special child in my life: _____ (insert name).

I pray that he (she) will come to know you personally as Savior, Lord, and Friend, and will walk closely with you all the days of his (her) life, for it's not enough to be raised in church, and it's not enough to hear about you in one's youth.

I pray this child will have a fresh, personal encounter with you and will walk with you all the days of his (her) life.

I ask you, O God, to reveal your truths in his (her) life.

I pray you enable him (her) to love truth and desire to be a person of honesty.

I pray that you would lead _____ by your truth, and help him (her) be quick to discern truth from falsehood.

I also pray that your church will be a beacon of truth to children worldwide, and that nothing will hinder the children from coming to you. Amen.

> 1 Kings 15:5; Job 42:5; Psalm 27:4; 1 Kings 3:9; Matthew 19:14.

## MONDAY: Make Fast the Breastplate of Righteousness

*Lord, I come before you as your beloved child, and I pray for these children whom I love:*

Date: _____ Names: _____

Date: _____ Names: _____

Date: _____ Names: _____

Date: _____ Names: _____

## Scriptures

*Lord, your Word teaches…*

> Stand firm then…with the breastplate of righteousness in place (Ephesians 6:14).

> Come, my children, listen to me;
>     I will teach you the fear of the LORD.
>                              (Psalm 34:11)

## Daily Prayer Openers (for ourselves or others; see pages 72-73)

## Armor Prayer

Lord,

- I pray on this Monday that you "make fast the breastplate of righteousness," especially on the children of this world.
- I pray that you protect them from unrighteous people, and guard them against anyone that would abuse, harm, or mislead them.
- They are so fragile, vulnerable, and naive; please put around them a hedge of protection.
- I also bring before you a particular child: _____.
- I ask you to put your armor on and around her (his) heart, for the heart is the wellspring of life.
- The heart can be as firm as stone or as soft as wax; it can be a place of mischief or stirred by noble themes; the heart can be full of pain or overflowing with joy.
- The heart is a deep place that can turn toward you or toward evil;
    O Lord, turn _____'s heart toward you.
- I pray that you would be the strength of her (his) heart.
- I pray that she (he) would not be deceived by her (his) own heart, for your Word tells us that our hearts are deceptive.
- I pray that you would give _____ a deep desire to live a life of honor, integrity, and righteousness, to live a life that pleases you, O God.

I pray this in the name of the King of Righteousness. Amen.

> 2 Peter 2:5; Job 1:10; Psalm 22:14; Psalm 45:1; Proverbs 16:21-22; Job 41:24; Psalm 28:3; Psalm 55:4; Acts 14:17; Psalm 64:6; Hebrews 3:12; Psalm 73:26; Jeremiah 17:9; Isaiah 32:1.

## TUESDAY: Tread in the Shoes of Peace

*Lord, I come before you as your beloved child, and I pray for these children whom I love:*

Date: _____ Names: _____

Date: _____ Names: _____

Date: _____ Names: _____

Date: _____ Names: _____

## Scriptures

*Lord, your Word teaches…*

> Stand firm then…with your feet fitted with the readiness that comes from the gospel of peace (Ephesians 6:14-15).

> "Blessed are the peacemakers,
>     for they will be called children of God."
>                         (Matthew 5:9)

## Daily Prayer Openers (for ourselves or others; see pages 72-73)

## Armor Prayer

Lord,

I pray on this Tuesday that you help the children in our world put on your "shoes of peace," so they may live quiet and peaceful lives in a world filled with noise, confusion, and conflict.

I plead for children who live in nations suffering under the ravages of war, that you protect them from harm, disease, abuse, and other forms of evil.

Teach them to be peacemakers in school, in their neighborhoods, and at home, for peacemakers will be blessed and called your children, O God.

I also pray specifically today for a child I care deeply about: may you put on _____ your shoes of peace.

May he (she) be quick to listen, slow to speak, and slow to anger; may he (she) be filled with your grace and truth, and have a discerning heart to walk in "the shoes of peace."

May he (she) mature to be very skilled at conflict resolution, for peacemakers who sow in peace reap a harvest of righteousness.

May God the Father and the Lord Jesus Christ fill him (her) with grace, mercy, and peace, in all truth and love.

And may _____ have spiritual peace with you, O God, and confidence of his (her) eternal salvation, forever and ever. Amen.

> 1 Timothy 2:2; Matthew 5:9; James 1:19; John 1:14; 1 Kings 3:9; James 3:18; 2 John 3.

## WEDNESDAY: Wield the Shield of Faith

*Lord, I come before you as your beloved child, and I pray for these children whom I love:*

Date: _____ Names: _____

Date: _____ Names: _____

Date: _____ Names: _____

Date: _____ Names: _____

## Scriptures

*Lord, your Word teaches…*

> Stand firm then…[and] take up the shield of faith, with which you can extinguish all the flaming arrows of the evil one (Ephesians 6:14,16).

> But Jesus called the children to him and said, "Let the little children come to me, and do not hinder them, for the kingdom of God belongs to such as these" (Luke 18:16).

## Daily Prayer Openers (for ourselves or others; see pages 72-73)

## Armor Prayer

Lord,

I pray on this Wednesday that you help the children in our world "wield the shield of faith" so they may live faith-filled lives in a world of unfaithfulness.

I pray for children who are being taught in classrooms and schools by unbelievers, that you protect their minds and plant your seed of faith in their hearts.

May they grow to understand that everyone has faith, and that those who claim to have no faith merely have faith in themselves, which is the most unstable, unproven, and dangerous faith of all.

For you love the just and will not forsake your faithful ones, and faithful people will be richly blessed.

I also pray specifically today for a child I care deeply about: may you put on _____ your "shield of faith."

May he (she) have the faith of Abel, whom you commended; may he (she) be like Enoch, who walked with you in faith; may he (she) be like Noah, who walked faithfully with you; and may he (she) walk in the faith of Moses, who talked with you as one does with a friend.

And may _____ have faith in the assurance of his (her)
eternal salvation, in you, O God, forever and ever.

I pray this in the Faithful and True name of Jesus. Amen.

> Romans 1:17; Luke 8:15; Psalm 101:3; Psalm 37:28; Proverbs
> 28:20; Hebrews 11:4; Genesis 5:24; Genesis 6:9; Exodus 33:11;
> 1 John 4:17; Psalm 23:6; Revelation 19:11.

## THURSDAY: Think Within the Helmet of Salvation

*Lord, I come before you as your beloved child, and I pray for these children whom I love:*

Date: _____ Names: _____

Date: _____ Names: _____

Date: _____ Names: _____

Date: _____ Names: _____

## Scriptures

*Lord, your Word teaches...*

> Stand firm then...Take the helmet of salvation (Ephesians
> 6:14,17).

> The disciples were amazed at his words. But Jesus said again,
> "Children, how hard it is to enter the kingdom of God!..."
> The disciples were even more amazed, and said to each
> other, "Who then can be saved?" (Mark 10:24,26).

## Daily Prayer Openers (for ourselves or others; see pages 72-73)

## Armor Prayer

Lord,

I pray on this Thursday that you help the children in our world learn to "think within your helmet of salvation," so their minds and thoughts will be protected in a world of mental chaos.

I pray for children who watch countless hours of TV and movies, that you guard their minds and prevent the enemy from planting seeds of impurity.

May they grow to understand that there is a battle going on for their minds, and those who claim to have all the answers are deceiving themselves.

This is a very difficult deception to overcome, because those in darkness do not know what makes them stumble.

I also pray specifically today for a child I care deeply about: may you put on _____ your "helmet of salvation."

Give her (him) a willing mind, for you search every heart and understand every desire and every thought.

Give her (him) a humble mind, not puffed up with her (his) own idle notions, faithless thoughts, or false beliefs.

And may _____ have the assurance that she (he) is saved by grace, through faith.

May she (he) grasp that this is not from herself (himself), but it is a gift from you; may she (he) become completely convinced that we are not saved by works, so that no one can boast.

And may _____ understand that she (he) is your handiwork, created in Christ Jesus to do good works, which you prepared in advance for her (him) to do. Amen.

> 1 John 1:8; Proverbs 4:19; 1 Chronicles 28:9; Colossians 2:18; Romans 3:21-24; Romans 6:23; Ephesians 2:8-9; Ephesians 2:10.

## FRIDAY: Fight with the Sword of the Spirit

*Lord, I come before you as your beloved child, and I pray for these children whom I love:*

Date: _____ Names: _____

Date: _____ Names: _____

Date: _____ Names: _____

Date: _____ Names: _____

## Scriptures

*Lord, your Word teaches...*

> Stand firm then...Take the sword of the Spirit, which is the word of God (Ephesians 6:14,17).

> Then he opened their minds so they could understand the Scriptures (Luke 24:45).

## Daily Prayer Openers (for ourselves or others; see pages 72-73)

## Armor Prayer

Lord,

I pray on this Friday that you help the children in our world "fight with the sword of the Spirit" so they may take their stand in a world filled with spiritual warfare.

I pray you would plant your Word in their hearts and like a mustard seed it would grow large and healthy.

I pray children today might come to firmly believe that your Word is trustworthy, logical, and factual.

Help them believe from the top of their heads to the tips of their toes, that trusting and obeying your Word is the smartest thing they will ever do.

I pray specifically today for a child I care deeply about: may you put on _____ "the sword of the Spirit."

Open her (his) eyes that she (he) might see the wonderful things in your Law.

Help her (him) grasp that your Word is the best lamp for her (his) feet, and the best light to guide her (his) path.

I pray she (he) would have the wisdom to hide your Word in her (his) heart, that she (he) might not sin against you.

Turn _____'s heart toward your statutes, and not toward selfish gain.

O Lord, great peace have those who love your law, and nothing can make them stumble.

I pray in the name of Jesus, the Word himself. Amen.

> Ephesians 6:12; Luke 13:19; Psalm 19:7; Psalm 119:18; Psalm 119:105; Psalm 119:11; Psalm 119:36; Psalm 119:165; John 1:1.

## SATURDAY: Steadfastly Pray in the Spirit

*Lord, I come before you as your beloved child, and I pray for these children whom I love:*

Date: _____ Names: _____

Date: _____ Names: _____

Date: _____ Names: _____

Date: _____ Names: _____

## Scriptures

*Lord, your Word teaches…*

Stand firm then…And pray in the Spirit on all occasions with all kinds of prayers and requests. With this in mind, be alert and always keep on praying for all the Lord's people (Ephesians 6:14,18).

When it was time to leave, we left and continued on our way. All of them, including wives and children, accompanied us out of the city, and there on the beach we knelt to pray (Acts 21:5).

## Daily Prayer Openers (for ourselves or others; see pages 72-73)

### Armor Prayer

Lord,

I pray on this Saturday that you help the children in our world steadfastly rest and "pray in the Spirit."

Kids today will step into a spiritual battle zone; they will have the flaming arrows of the enemy launched at them all day long.

The enemy is relentless, and his only desire is to kill and destroy them.

I pray that you would put on them your full armor, O God, so they can take their stand against the evil one.

I pray specifically today for a child I care deeply about: may you help _____ steadfastly rest and "pray in the Spirit."

Open her (his) eyes, that she (he) might see the power of prayer.

Give her (him) the desire to speak with you all day long, to have a conversation with you, in her (his) heart and mind, that never ends.

And may _____ learn to rest in you; may she (he) rest every day in your love, grace, and presence.

May every day be a Sabbath for her (him), every day a day of worship, praise, and thankfulness, as she (he) rests from works-righteousness, knowing there is no way she (he) can earn your grace.

May she (he) rest in you, Jesus, Lord of the Sabbath, forever and ever. Amen.

> John 10:10; Ephesians 6:11; James 5:16; 1 Thessalonians 5:16-18; Hebrews 4:3; Romans 12:1; Ephesians 2:8; Matthew 12:8.

# WEEK SEVEN

## Praying for Men

### Instructions for Week Seven

Men are under spiritual attack in our society today. TV shows mock men in general (think Homer Simpson), and both marriage and fatherhood are being redefined (think *Modern Family*). Gender roles are not just confused but denied, and equality is the reigning value. The result: many men today simply don't know what it means to be masculine, to be a husband, or to be a father. To put it bluntly, they don't know how to be a man. Fortunately, the Bible provides the answers our society needs, and the power of prayer can help men discover biblical manhood and experience it in their own lives.

If you're a woman, you may at first assume these prayers don't apply to you and you'll be tempted to skip this week. I urge you to reconsider. After all, don't you know some men who need prayer? A brother, father, cousin, coworker, classmate, church friend? Plus, some women feel very helpless when it comes to the men or boys in their lives. What can they do to help? Prayer is one answer, and persistent, targeted prayer is powerful. So ladies, give this a week a try; as you see the men in your lives slowly transform, it may become your favorite week. (But if it's just not your cup of tea, feel free to skip to next week.)

One final comment: men may finally find, during this week, an enjoyable way to pray. Armor, after all, is something most men can relate with. It's masculine. It's military. It's tough. Whereas men sometimes feel pressured in churches to act in touchy-feely, feminine ways, this allows men to draw close to God in a way that doesn't compromise manhood. So whether you are male or female, let's confidently approach the throne of grace and bring the men in our lives to God in prayer. They will receive mercy and grace in their time of need—which is now (Hebrews 4:16).

## SUNDAY: Strap on the Belt of Truth

*Lord, today I want to bring before you in prayer these men (boys):*

Date: _____ Names: _____

(Use the following spaces for future weeks when you cycle again through these prayers.)

Date: _____ Names: _____

Date: _____ Names: _____

Date: _____ Names: _____

## Scriptures

*Lord, your Word teaches...*

> Stand firm then, with the belt of truth buckled around your waist (Ephesians 6:14).

> For You have girded me with strength for battle;
> You have subdued under me those who rose up against me.
> (2 Samuel 22:40 NASB)

## Daily Prayer Openers (for ourselves or others; see pages 72-73)

## Armor Prayer

Lord,

It's Sunday, so it's a reminder to "strap on the belt of truth," which means you are preparing us for battle.

Today I want to pray for a man (boy) I care about named _____, that he truly will become the man you created him to be.

And so on this day, I ask you to ready him for the battles that
  await him, by girding around him your truth, wisdom, and
  knowledge.

As you instructed Job to gird up his loins like a man, I pray you
  help him become the masculine man you created him to be.

As you led Ehud to gird and hide his sword against his thigh, I ask
  you to gird and truly hide your Word within his heart.

As you helped Elijah gird up his loins and race ahead of Ahab, help
  him run with endurance the race set before him.

As you girded and armed David with strength for battle, and made
  his adversaries bow at his feet, so I ask you to give him true
  strength and victory today.

As you commanded Jeremiah to gird up his loins and speak all that
  you had commanded him to say, so allow him to be ready to
  stand in Truth and speak for you today.

And as Jesus girded a towel about his waist and washed his followers' feet, so too may he be like his master, willing to humble
  himself and follow Jesus' example by truly serving others.

Lord, allow him to be your man, belted with truth, today. Amen.

> 2 Samuel 22:40; Job 38:3; 40:7; Judges 3:16; Psalm 119:11;
> 1 Kings 18:46; Hebrews 12:1; Psalm 18:39; Jeremiah 1:17; John
> 13:4.

## MONDAY: Make Fast the Breastplate of Righteousness

*Lord, today I want to bring before you in prayer these men (boys):*

Date: _____ Names: _____

Date: _____ Names: _____

Date: _____ Names: _____

Date: _____ Names: _____

### Scriptures

*Lord, your Word teaches...*

> Stand firm then...with the breastplate of righteousness in place (Ephesians 6:14).

> He put on righteousness as his breastplate,
>     and the helmet of salvation on his head;
> he put on the garments of vengeance
>     and wrapped himself in zeal as in a cloak.
>                     (Isaiah 59:17)

### Daily Prayer Openers (for ourselves or others; see pages 72-73)

### Armor Prayer

Lord,

I pray on this Monday that you "make fast the breastplate of righteousness," that _____ would become the righteous man you created him to be.

As you made and put a breastplate and ephod on the high priest, I pray you put your breastplate of righteousness on him so he can be a worthy priest for his family.

You put "the Urim and Thummim" in the high priest's breastplate to help him fathom your will and discern your ways; so give him the wisdom to lead his family in your paths.

Help him follow the wisdom of Solomon, who said, "Above all else, guard your heart, for everything you do flows from it."

In addition, I ask you to fasten on him the breastplate of faith and love, so he can be a faithful and loving servant in your kingdom.

I pray this in the name of the King of Righteousness. Amen.

> Exodus 28:4; 1 Peter 2:5; Leviticus 8:8; 1 Timothy 3:5; Proverbs 4:23; 1 Thessalonians 5:8.

## TUESDAY: Tread in the Shoes of Peace

*Lord, today I want to bring before you in prayer these men (boys):*

Date: _____ Names: _____

Date: _____ Names: _____

Date: _____ Names: _____

Date: _____ Names: _____

## Scriptures

*Lord, your Word teaches…*

> Stand firm then…with your feet fitted with the readiness that comes from the gospel of peace (Ephesians 6:14-15).

> "How beautiful are the feet of those who bring good news!" (Romans 10:15).

## Daily Prayer Openers (for ourselves or others; see pages 72-73)

## Armor Prayer

Lord,

It's impossible to stand firm without solid footwear, so on

this Tuesday I ask you to put your "shoes of peace" on
_____.

Then he can move securely on this dangerous battlefield, able even to tread on lions and snakes.

Give him warrior's boots that can be used in battle, but let them be boots of peace to help resolve conflicts and disagreements.

In a world full of discord and enmity, allow him to be a peacemaker.

Help him to always be on guard and to stand firm in the faith, to be courageous and to be strong, for we know it is you, O God, who gives us the strength to stand firm.

Allow him, a warrior for Christ, to always stand firm.

Let nothing move him except the movement of your Spirit.

Let him always give himself fully to the work of the Lord, because we know that his labor for you is not in vain.

As you yourself said, "The one who stands firm to the end will be saved." Amen.

> Ephesians 6:15; Psalm 91:13; James 3:18; 1 Corinthians 16:13;
> 2 Corinthians 1:21; Exodus 14:13; Acts 16:7; 1 Corinthians
> 15:58; Matthew 24:13; Mark 13:13.

## WEDNESDAY: Wield the Shield of Faith

*Lord, today I want to bring before you in prayer these men (boys):*

Date: _____ Names: _____

Date: _____ Names: _____

Date: _____ Names: _____

Date: _____ Names: _____

## Scriptures

*Lord, your Word teaches…*

> Stand firm then…[and] take up the shield of faith, with
> which you can extinguish all the flaming arrows of the evil
> one (Ephesians 6:14,16).

> Prepare your shields, both large and small,
> and march out for battle!
> (Jeremiah 46:3)

## Daily Prayer Openers (for ourselves or others; see pages 72-73)

### Armor Prayer

Lord,

It's Wednesday, and the flaming arrows of the evil one are already
launched and flying toward those I love.

They are in constant danger.

So on this Wednesday I ask you to help _____ "wield the
shield of faith."

Help him remember your promise to Abram: "Do not be afraid. I
am your shield, your very great reward."

Remind him of the Song of Moses,
"Let the beloved of the LORD rest secure in him, for he shields
him all day long, and the one the LORD loves rests between his
shoulders."

Give him the confidence of David, who sang,
"But you, LORD, are a shield around me, my glory, the One who
lifts my head high."

Place him in a body of brave believers, your church, where he can
prepare his shields, both large and small, and march out for
battle.

Help him stand side by side with others even during times of trouble, and may he never be part of any divisive or insubordinate rebellion.

And I thank you that through faith, we are shielded by your power until the coming of the salvation that is ready to be revealed in the last time. Amen.

> 2 Corinthians 11:26; Genesis 15:1; Deuteronomy 33:12;
> Psalm 3:3; Jeremiah 46:3; Hebrews 10:33; 1 Timothy 3:10;
> 1 Peter 1:5.

## THURSDAY: Think Within the Helmet of Salvation

*Lord, today I want to bring before you in prayer these men (boys):*

Date: _____ Names: _____

Date: _____ Names: _____

Date: _____ Names: _____

Date: _____ Names: _____

## Scriptures

*Lord, your Word teaches...*

Stand firm then... Take the helmet of salvation (Ephesians 6:14,17).

Uzziah had a well-trained army... [he] provided shields, spears, helmets, coats of armor, bows and slingstones for the entire army (2 Chronicles 26:11,14).

## Daily Prayer Openers (for ourselves or others; see pages 72-73)

### Armor Prayer

Lord,

You are our light and our salvation—whom shall we fear?

You are the stronghold of our lives—of whom shall we be afraid?

So on this Thursday I ask you to help _____ "think within the helmet of salvation," for his mind is a battlefield where the enemy often wins.

As King Uzziah gave helmets to protect the heads of his soldiers, so I ask you to provide him a spiritually protective helmet.

How long must he wrestle with his thoughts and day after day have sorrow in his heart?

I realize that his thoughts are not your thoughts; neither are your ways his ways.

As the heavens are higher than the earth, so are your ways higher than his ways and your thoughts above his.

Give him the very mind of Christ; put your law in his mind and write it on his heart.

I ask you to put the hope of salvation on him as a helmet, and help him have the assurance of the knowledge of salvation. Amen.

> Psalm 27:1; 1 Peter 5:8; 2 Chronicles 26:14; Psalm 13:2; Isaiah 55:8; Isaiah 55:9; 1 Corinthians 2:16; Jeremiah 31:33; 1 Thessalonians 5:8; 1 John 3:19.

## FRIDAY: Fight with the Sword of the Spirit

*Lord, today I want to bring before you in prayer these men (boys):*

Date: _____ Names: _____

Date: _____ Names: _____

Date: _____ Names: _____

Date: _____ Names: _____

## Scriptures

*Lord, your Word teaches…*

> Stand firm then…Take the sword of the Spirit, which is the word of God (Ephesians 6:14,17).

> Gird your sword on your side, you mighty one;
> clothe yourself with splendor and majesty.
> (Psalm 45:3)

## Daily Prayer Openers (for ourselves or others; see pages 72-73)

## Armor Prayer

Lord,

I ask you on this Friday to help _____ "fight with the sword of the Spirit."

May he become a warrior of your Word; give him knowledge and insight into your Word, that he may defeat the ancient foe who wars against him.

As your cherubim flashed a sword back and forth to protect Eden, so help him wield the sword of your Spirit to protect your flock.

As Joshua overcame the enemy army with the sword, so let him overcome the evil forces that are arrayed against him.

As you opened Balaam's eyes to see the angel's drawn sword, so I ask you to open his eyes to the power of your Word.

As Jonathan befriended David and gave him his sword, so I ask you to befriend _____ and protect him with your Word.

And as Jesus himself responded to the temptations of the devil, "Man shall not live on bread alone, but on every word that comes from the mouth of God," so allow him to feed on and live by your Word.

O Lord, please arm him with your truth; set his heart on your laws; help him hold fast to your statutes; do not let him be put to shame. Amen.

Matthew 4:10; Genesis 3:24; Exodus 17:13; Numbers 22:31; 1 Samuel 18:4; Matthew 4:4; Psalm 119:30; Psalm 119:31.

## SATURDAY: Steadfastly Pray in the Spirit

*Lord, today I want to bring before you in prayer these men (boys):*

Date: _____ Names: _____

Date: _____ Names: _____

Date: _____ Names: _____

Date: _____ Names: _____

## Scriptures

*Lord, your Word teaches...*

Stand firm then...And pray in the Spirit on all occasions with all kinds of prayers and requests. With this in mind, be alert and always keep on praying for all the Lord's people (Ephesians 6:14,18).

Trust in him at all times, you people;
  pour out your hearts to him,
  for God is our refuge.
                    (Psalm 62:8)


## Daily Prayer Openers (for ourselves or others; see pages 72-73)

## Armor Prayer

Lord,

Even brave soldiers are afraid at times, and courage is not the absence of fear but action in the face of fear.

So on this Saturday I ask you to give _____ the courage to rest in you and your safety.

I ask you to help him "steadfastly pray in the Spirit"; allow him to rest beneath the shadow of your wings.

You are his hiding place; you will protect him from trouble and surround him with songs of deliverance.

In a world full of unrest and distress, may he choose to rest in you.

In you he trusts, O God; do not let him be put to shame, nor let his enemies triumph over him.

Many are the woes of the wicked, but your unfailing love surrounds him because he trusts in you.

Some trust in chariots and horses, but he trusts in the name of the Lord his God.

When he is afraid, remind him to trust in you; in you, whose Word he praises—in you he trusts and will not be afraid.

What can mere mortals do to him? Amen.

> Joshua 1:9; Deuteronomy 12:10; Ruth 2:12; Psalm 32:7; Psalm 62:5; Psalm 25:1; Psalm 25:2; Psalm 32:10; Psalm 20:7; Psalm 56:3; Psalm 56:4.

# WEEK EIGHT

## Praying for Women

### Instructions for Week Eight

This week, we will accomplish two tasks: first, we will pray specifically for the women in our lives; second, we will learn to pray through entire passages of Scripture.

Many Christians read the Bible daily but don't take advantage of those daily readings as prayer guides. This week, each day we will learn how to pray through a section of Scripture, which relates to the armor of the day. By the time we finish praying for three or four women, we will be on our way to memorizing the Scripture, which is a terrific added benefit.

By now you are probably noticing that your prayers have been saturated in the Word of God, and God's own vocabulary and promises are gradually becoming your own. But the journey of praying the armor of God has just begun, because the whole Bible also can become a prayer guide. After following the guided prayers this week, try to pray your daily Bible readings. You will find most passages in the Bible can also become meaningful prayers.

---

### SUNDAY: Strap on the Belt of Truth

*Lord, today I will pray for these women (girls) in my life:*

Date: _____ Names: _____

(Use the following spaces for future weeks when you cycle again through these prayers.)

Date: _____ Names: _____

Date: _____ Names: _____

Date: _____ Names: _____

## Scriptures

*Lord, your Word teaches...*

> Stand firm then, with the belt of truth buckled around your waist (Ephesians 6:14).

> God, who said, "Let light shine out of darkness," made his light shine in our hearts to give us the light of the knowledge of God's glory displayed in the face of Christ (2 Corinthians 4:6).

## Daily Prayer Openers (for ourselves or others; see pages 72-73)

## Armor Prayer

Lord,

It's Sunday, so once again I ask you, O God, to "strap the belt of truth" on the women (girls) in my life.

I pray that they may grasp the truth of what the apostle Paul prayed for his friends in Ephesus:

"I keep asking that the God of our Lord Jesus Christ, the glorious Father, may give [_____ insert name] the Spirit of wisdom and revelation, so that [she] may know him better.

I pray that the eyes of [her] heart may be enlightened in order that [she] may know the hope to which he has called [her], the riches of his glorious inheritance in his holy people, and his incomparably great power for us who believe."

May _____ grasp these truths, which come only through knowing you. Amen.

Ephesians 1:17-19a.

## MONDAY: Make Fast the Breastplate of Righteousness

*Lord, today I will pray for these women (girls) in my life:*

Date: _____ Names: _____

Date: _____ Names: _____

Date: _____ Names: _____

Date: _____ Names: _____

## Scriptures
*Lord, your Word teaches…*

> Stand firm then…with the breastplate of righteousness in place (Ephesians 6:14).

> May the mountains bring prosperity to the people,
>     the hills the fruit of righteousness.
>                 (Psalm 72:3)

## Daily Prayer Openers (for ourselves or others; see pages 72-73)
## Armor Prayer

Lord,

I pray on this Monday that you "make fast the breastplate of righteousness," and I pray for the women (girls) in my life, as the apostle Paul prayed for his friends:
"And this is my prayer: that [_____'s] love may abound more and more in knowledge and depth of insight, so that [she]

may be able to discern what is best and may be pure and blameless for the day of Christ, filled with the fruit of righteousness
that comes through Jesus Christ—to the glory and praise of
God."

Lord, may _____ experience the righteousness that you
  alone can give. Amen.

> Philippians 1:9-11.

## TUESDAY: Tread in the Shoes of Peace

*Lord, today I will pray for these women (or girls) in my life:*

Date: _____ Names: _____

Date: _____ Names: _____

Date: _____ Names: _____

Date: _____ Names: _____

## Scriptures

*Lord, your Word teaches...*

> Stand firm then...with your feet fitted with the readiness
> that comes from the gospel of peace (Ephesians 6:14-15).

> How good and pleasant it is
>   when God's people live together in unity!
>                     (Psalm 133:1)

## Daily Prayer Openers (for ourselves or others; see pages 72-73)

## Armor Prayer

Lord,

  I pray on this Tuesday that you help us "tread in the shoes of peace," and I pray for the women (girls) in my life, as the Lord Jesus prayed for us.

I pray for those _____ (insert names) who have believed in Jesus through the apostles' message, that all of us may be one, just as you, Father, are in Jesus and Jesus is in you.

May _____ also be in you, O God, so that the world may believe that you sent Jesus.

For Jesus has given us the glory that you gave him, that we may be one as you, O God, are One.

Jesus in us and you, Father, in Jesus, so that we may be brought to complete unity.

Then the world will know that you sent Jesus and love _____ even as you love Jesus.

Lord, may these women (girls), _____, experience the peace and togetherness that oneness with you brings. Amen.

John 17:20-23.

## WEDNESDAY: Wield the Shield of Faith

*Lord, today I will pray for these women (girls) in my life:*

Date: _____ Names: _____

Date: _____ Names: _____

Date: _____ Names: _____

Date: _____ Names: _____

## Scriptures

*Lord, your Word teaches…*

> Stand firm then…[and] take up the shield of faith, with which you can extinguish all the flaming arrows of the evil one (Ephesians 6:14,16).

> The only thing that counts is faith expressing itself through love (Galatians 5:6).

## Daily Prayer Openers (for ourselves or others; see pages 72-73)

## Armor Prayer

Lord,

It's Wednesday, so I ask you to help the women (girls) in my life "wield the shield of faith."

And I pray with the apostle Paul as he prayed for his friends in Ephesus:

"I pray that out of his glorious riches he may strengthen _____ with power through his Spirit in [her] inner being, so that Christ may dwell in [her] heart through faith.

And I pray that [she], being rooted and established in love, may have power, together with all the Lord's holy people, to grasp how wide and long and high and deep is the love of Christ, and to know this love that surpasses knowledge—that [she] may be filled to the measure of all the fullness of God.

Now to him who is able to do immeasurably more than all we ask or imagine, according to his power that is at work within us, to him be glory in the church and in Christ Jesus throughout all generations, for ever and ever!"

Lord, may _____'s shield of faith in you grow higher, deeper, and wider. Amen.

Ephesians 3:16-21.

## THURSDAY: Think Within the Helmet of Salvation

*Lord, today I will pray for these women (or girls) in my life:*

Date: _____ Names: _____

Date: _____ Names: _____

Date: _____ Names: _____

Date: _____ Names: _____

### Scriptures

*Lord, your Word teaches…*

> Stand firm then…Take the helmet of salvation (Ephesians 6:14,17).

> But since we belong to the day, let us be sober, putting on faith and love as a breastplate, and the hope of salvation as a helmet (1 Thessalonians 5:8).

### Daily Prayer Openers (for ourselves or others; see pages 72-73)

### Armor Prayer

Lord,

It's Thursday, so I ask you to help the women (girls) in my life "think within the helmet of salvation."

And I pray with the half-brother of Jesus as he prayed for his friends to keep their focus on the Savior:

"To him who is able to keep _____ from stumbling and to present [her] before his glorious presence without fault and with great joy—to the only God our Savior be glory, majesty, power and authority, through Jesus Christ our Lord, before all ages, now and forevermore!"

Lord, may _____, together with others in your church,
    put on the helmet of salvation, who is Christ our Savior. Amen.

    Jude 24-25.

## FRIDAY: Fight with the Sword of the Spirit

*Lord, today I will pray for these women (girls) in my life:*

Date: _____ Names: _____

Date: _____ Names: _____

Date: _____ Names: _____

Date: _____ Names: _____

## Scriptures

*Lord, your Word teaches...*

> Stand firm then...Take the sword of the Spirit, which is
> the word of God (Ephesians 6:14,17).

> All Scripture is God-breathed and is useful for teaching,
> rebuking, correcting and training in righteousness (2 Tim-
> othy 3:16).

## Daily Prayer Openers (for ourselves or others; see pages 72-73)

## Armor Prayer

Lord,

    It's Friday, so I ask you to strengthen and empower the women
        (girls) in my life to "fight with the sword of the Spirit."

    And I pray with David, who wrote this beautiful song that declares your glory as revealed in the Scriptures, which is the sword of the Spirit:

"The law of the LORD is perfect, refreshing the soul [Lord, please help _____ find refreshment from your Word].

The statutes of the LORD are trustworthy, making wise the simple [Lord, please help her learn wisdom from your Word].

The precepts of the LORD are right, giving joy to the heart [Lord, please help her be filled with joy from your Word].

The commands of the LORD are radiant, giving light to the eyes [Lord, please help her see the brilliance of your Word].

The fear of the LORD is pure, enduring forever [Lord, please help her learn purity from your Word].

The decrees of the LORD are firm, and all of them are righteous [Lord, please help her find a firm foundation in your Word].

They are more precious than gold, than much pure gold [Lord, please help her value your Word above all treasures]; they are sweeter than honey, than honey from the honeycomb [Lord, please help her find sweet nourishment in your Word].

By them your servant is warned; in keeping them there is great reward [Lord, please help her heed the warnings from your Word]."

Lord, may you strengthen her with your Word, the sword of the Spirit. Amen.

> Psalm 19:7-11.

## SATURDAY: Steadfastly Pray in the Spirit

*Lord, today I will pray for these women (girls) in my life:*

Date: _____ Names: _____

Date: _____ Names: _____

Date: _____ Names: _____

Date: _____ Names: _____

## Scriptures

*Lord, your Word teaches…*

> Stand firm then…And pray in the Spirit on all occasions with all kinds of prayers and requests. With this in mind, be alert and always keep on praying for all the saints (Ephesians 6:14,18).

> In the same way, the Spirit helps us in our weakness. We do not know what we ought to pray for, but the Spirit himself intercedes for us through wordless groans (Romans 8:26).

## Daily Prayer Openers (for ourselves or others; see pages 72-73)

## Armor Prayer

Lord,

It's Saturday, so I ask you to help the women (girls) in my life "steadfastly pray in the Spirit."

And I pray with the Lord Jesus, as he taught his followers to pray with these words:

"Our Father who is in heaven [Lord, let _____ never doubt you exist and rule from heaven],

Hallowed be Your name [Lord, let _____ never forget that you are holy and not to be taken for granted].

Your kingdom come [Lord, may you take over ownership and management of _____'s life].

Your will be done [Lord, show _____ what your will is, and give her the wisdom to follow it],

On earth as it is in heaven [Lord, take charge of _____'s life, as you rule in heaven].

Give us this day our daily bread [Lord, provide for _____'s daily needs, and help her always thank you for your daily provision].

And forgive us our debts [Lord Jesus Christ, have mercy on _____, a sinner],

as we also have forgiven our debtors [Lord Jesus, help _____ show others the same mercy you have shown her].

And do not lead us into temptation [Lord, lead _____ away from tempting places, people, and thoughts],

but deliver us from evil [Lord, protect _____ from the evil one who is trying to tempt and destroy her].

For yours is the kingdom and the power and the glory, forever [Lord, may _____ praise and honor you, forever and ever]."

Lord, allow her to pray steadfastly as Jesus taught, which is to never give up trusting in God's presence, love, and power. Amen.

Matthew 6:9-13 NASB.

# WEEK NINE

## Praying for Prodigals

### Instructions for Week Nine

Do you know a person who has grown lukewarm in his or her relationship with God? Who has wandered from the path of faith? Who has been enticed by the false promises of this world, has been bankrupted morally, financially, or spiritually, or has hit (or is close to hitting) rock bottom in life? In other words, do you know anyone who is a prodigal?

Our hearts break for the prodigals we love, but what can we do? We can't force them to come back to God or to mend their broken ways. We can't live their lives for them, and we can't open their eyes to the danger of their paths (Lord knows we've tried!). If you love a prodigal, you probably feel a deep sense of helplessness and frustration. We want to help but feel powerless.

But we are not helpless—we can pray! We can pray because God loves these people more than we do, and his will is for them to come to repentance (2 Peter 3:9). There is power in patient prayer, and the grace of the Lord is abundant.

This is why Jesus taught what is often referred to as the Parable of the Prodigal Son, recorded in Luke 15:11-24. *Prodigal* means "lavish or extravagant," which is how the wayward son spent his inheritance. But there is someone in the parable even more prodigious than the son: the father. Seen in this light, the real point of the parable is the amazing love, generosity, and grace of the father. This is clearly a story about our exceptional heavenly Father—so much so that perhaps it should be called the Parable of the Prodigal Father.

Keeping this in mind, let's approach our Prodigal God, asking him to pour his prodigious, bountiful mercy on those we love and to draw the wayward back into his forgiving arms. This week, we will be guided by this parable as we pray the armor of God onto the lives of those we love.

## SUNDAY: Strap on the Belt of Truth

*Lord, today I ask you to work in the lives of these people who have wandered:*

Date: _____ Names: _____

(Use the following spaces for future weeks when you cycle again through these prayers.)

Date: _____ Names: _____

Date: _____ Names: _____

Date: _____ Names: _____

## Scriptures

*Lord, your Word teaches…*

> Stand firm then, with the belt of truth buckled around your waist (Ephesians 6:14).

> "There was a man who had two sons. The younger one said to his father, 'Father, give me my share of the estate.' So he divided his property between them. Not long after that, the younger son got together all he had, set off for a distant country and there squandered his wealth in wild living" (Luke 15:11-13).

## Daily Prayer Openers (for ourselves or others; see pages 72-73)

## Armor Prayer

Lord,

On this Sunday I pray for the prodigals who have wandered away from you, that you would mercifully "strap on them the belt of truth."

Your Word says that all of us like sheep have wandered, each of us has gone astray and turned to his own way.

I pray for _____ that you would help him (her) see the truth of his (her) situation: that the distant country is a place of sadness, pain, and misery; that wild living seems full of life for a time, but actually leads to death.

I ask that your truth would flood his (her) soul, so he (she) would realize he (she) is squandering his (her) life and decide to come home. Amen.

Isaiah 53:6.

## MONDAY: Make Fast the Breastplate of Righteousness

*Lord, today I ask you to work in the lives of these people who have wandered:*

Date: _____ Names: _____

Date: _____ Names: _____

Date: _____ Names: _____

Date: _____ Names: _____

## Scriptures

*Lord, your Word teaches…*

Stand firm then…with the breastplate of righteousness in place (Ephesians 6:14).

"After he had spent everything, there was a severe famine in that whole country, and he began to be in need. So he went and hired himself out to a citizen of that country, who sent him to his fields to feed pigs. He longed to fill his stomach with the pods that the pigs were eating, but no one gave him anything" (Luke 15:14-16).

## Daily Prayer Openers (for ourselves or others; see pages 72-73)

## Armor Prayer

Lord,

> On this Monday I pray for the prodigals who have wandered away from you, please "make fast on them your breastplate of righteousness."

> I pray for _____, that you would help her (him) feel spiritually famished.

> I pray there would be a deep hunger within her (his) heart, a longing for you that will be deeper than all other desires.

> I pray that every attempt _____ makes to fill the emptiness within would be unsuccessful.

> I pray she (he) would discover that life without you is empty, bestial, and hollow.

> I pray she (he) would hunger and thirst for your righteousness, and that she (he) would long to return to the warmth of your embrace and quickly come home to you. Amen.

## TUESDAY: Tread in the Shoes of Peace

*Lord, today I ask you to work in the lives of these people who have wandered:*

Date: _____ Names: _____

Date: _____ Names: _____

Date: _____ Names: _____

Date: _____ Names: _____

## Scriptures

*Lord, your Word teaches…*

> Stand firm then…with your feet fitted with the readiness that comes from the gospel of peace (Ephesians 6:14-15).

> "When he came to his senses, he said, 'How many of my father's hired servants have food to spare, and here I am starving to death! I will set out and go back to my father and say to him: Father, I have sinned against heaven and against you. I am no longer worthy to be called your son; make me like one of your hired servants.' So he got up and went to his father" (Luke 15:17-20).

## Daily Prayer Openers (for ourselves or others; see pages 72-73)

## Armor Prayer

Lord,

On this Tuesday I pray for the prodigals who have gone into the far country, that you would graciously put on them your "shoes of peace."

I pray for _____, that you would help her (him) come to her (his) senses.

May the scales of the devil's deceptions fall from her (his) eyes, and may she (he) realize that life is better with you, O Father, than apart from you.

May she (he) decide to be a peacemaker and make amends with you.

May you give her (him) the wisdom to humble herself (himself), and to approach you with repentance and confession.

As the prodigal son came to his senses, got up from the pit, and went home, please move in _____'s heart and lead her (him) home to you. Amen.

## WEDNESDAY: Wield the Shield of Faith

*Lord, today I ask you to work in the lives of these people who have wandered:*

Date: _____ Names: _____

Date: _____ Names: _____

Date: _____ Names: _____

Date: _____ Names: _____

## Scriptures

*Lord, your Word teaches…*

> Stand firm then…[and] take up the shield of faith, with which you can extinguish all the flaming arrows of the evil one (Ephesians 6:14,16).

> "But while he was still a long way off, his father saw him and was filled with compassion for him; he ran to his son, threw his arms around him and kissed him" (Luke 15:20).

## Daily Prayer Openers (for ourselves or others; see pages 72-73)

## Armor Prayer

Lord,

> On this Wednesday I pray for the prodigals who have strayed from your side, that you would generously allow them to "wield the shield of faith."

> I pray for _____, that you would grant him (her) the faith to believe you are merciful; the faith to trust that you are a loving and forgiving God; the faith to hope that if we confess our sins you are faithful and just to forgive us.

> I ask you to help him (her) see, even from a far distance away, that you desire to be reconciled, and you are running toward him (her), that your arms are outstretched to forgive and embrace,

and that your face is beaming with smiles of joy and tears of gladness.

Help him (her) to have the faith that a loving kiss awaits him (her), and that you long to tenderly welcome him (her) home. Amen.

1 John 1:9.

## THURSDAY: Think Within the Helmet of Salvation

*Lord, today I ask you to work in the lives of these people who have wandered:*

Date: _____ Names: _____

Date: _____ Names: _____

Date: _____ Names: _____

Date: _____ Names: _____

## Scriptures

*Lord, your Word teaches…*

> Stand firm then…Take the helmet of salvation (Ephesians 6:14,17).

> "The son said to him, 'Father, I have sinned against heaven and against you. I am no longer worthy to be called your son'" (Luke 15:21).

## Daily Prayer Openers (for ourselves or others; see pages 72-73)

## Armor Prayer

Lord,

On this Thursday I pray for the prodigals who have drifted from your presence, that you would enlighten them to "think within the helmet of salvation."

I pray for _____, that you would grant her (him) the
   wisdom to see the need of salvation; that being a pretty good
   person isn't good enough to get into heaven, because heaven is
   perfect and nothing impure will enter it.

Help _____ to understand there is no way she (he) is
   worthy to come home or deserving of forgiveness.

None of us is worthy to be called a son or daughter, and no one,
   including me, is able to earn your grace.

Help her (him) not to be deceived by the evil one, who has
   blinded the minds of so many people, misleading them to
   believe that you don't exist.

What a colossal, eternal mistake: to believe there is no God,
   heaven, or hell!

I pray that _____ would be saved, now and forevermore.
   Amen.

Revelation 21:27.

## FRIDAY: Fight with the Sword of the Spirit

*Lord, today I ask you to work in the lives of these people who have wandered:*

Date: _____ Names: _____

Date: _____ Names: _____

Date: _____ Names: _____

Date: _____ Names: _____

## Scriptures

*Lord, your Word teaches…*

Stand firm then…Take the sword of the Spirit, which is
the word of God (Ephesians 6:14,17).

"But the father said to his servants, 'Quick! Bring the best robe and put it on him. Put a ring on his finger and sandals on his feet. Bring the fattened calf and kill it. Let's have a feast and celebrate'" (Luke 15:22-23).

## Daily Prayer Openers (for ourselves or others; see pages 72-73)

### Armor Prayer

Lord,

On this Friday I pray for prodigals who are being deceived by the evil one, that you would equip them to "fight with the sword of the Spirit."

I pray for _____, that he (she) will learn to love and believe your Word, and decide that there is no wiser way to live than according to your Word.

Help him (her), in a blinding flash of insight, to see that you are the Word; you are the way, the truth, and the life; you are the good shepherd, the light of the world, the living bread.

You were in the beginning, you were with God, and you are God.

Help him (her) to realize that you were the fattened calf slain for him (her), that your death has purchased for him (her) eternal robes, rings, and sandals.

We will feast and celebrate eternally in heaven only if we believe in our heart and confess with our lips that you are Lord and Savior.

May you grant _____ the wisdom to do this soon. Amen.

> John 1:1; John 14:6; John 10:11; 8:12; 6:35; John 20:28; Romans 10:9.

## SATURDAY: Steadfastly Pray in the Spirit

*Lord, today I ask you to work in the lives of these people who have wandered:*

Date: _____ Names: _____

(Use the following spaces for future weeks when you cycle again through these prayers.)

Date: _____ Names: _____

Date: _____ Names: _____

Date: _____ Names: _____

### Scriptures

*Lord, your Word teaches…*

> Stand firm then…And pray in the Spirit on all occasions with all kinds of prayers and requests. With this in mind, be alert and always keep on praying for all the Lord's people (Ephesians 6:14,18).

> "'For this son of mine was dead and is alive again; he was lost and is found.' So they began to celebrate" (Luke 15:24).

### Daily Prayer Openers (for ourselves or others; see pages 72-73)

### Armor Prayer

Lord,

On this Saturday I pray for the prodigals coming home from the distant country, that you would enable them to rest by "steadfastly praying in the Spirit."

I pray for _____.

Please teach her (him) to relax and repose in you and your love.

I ask that she (he) would feel new life coming into her (his) body, soul, and spirit; that you would bring life to the valley of dry bones she (he) made.

I pray that _____ will learn to pray and communicate with you; that she (he) will learn to pray without ceasing
because you are ever with her (him).

Reveal to her (him) the incredible truth that she (he) is never alone,
because you will never leave her (him) or forsake her (him).

I ask that she (he), a person who once was lost, will never cease to
be amazed that she (he) has been found, welcomed home, and
fully restored in your family.

Your love and grace are wonders too marvelous for words. Amen.

Ezekiel 37:1-14; Hebrews 13:5.

# WEEK TEN

## Praying for Leaders

### Instructions for Week Ten

More people probably complain about leaders than pray for them. Yet the Bible tells us that we are to pray for leaders; in fact, it instructs that praying for leaders is one of the first things we should do: "I urge, then, first of all, that petitions, prayers, intercession and thanksgiving be made for all people—for kings and all those in authority, that we may live peaceful and quiet lives in all godliness and holiness" (1 Timothy 2:1-2).

Thanking God for the leaders in our world today will be a hard task for some of us. We may not have voted for these leaders, our values may be opposite theirs, and our opinions of them low. Nonetheless, we are urged to pray.

How can we manage this? First of all, it may help to remember that Paul wrote these words to Timothy when the world leaders were the despised Romans, who certainly held values and followed policies contrary to those of the Christian and Jewish communities. Second, this reminds us that God's ways are not our ways, and he often raises up and tears down both righteous and unrighteous leaders for his own purposes, which are unknown to us (Jeremiah 23:5; 50:9).

So on this last week of guided prayers, we will follow the apostle Paul's instructions to young Timothy, and we will pray for the leaders in our lives. Each day we will focus on a different set of leaders—local, state, national, business, school, missions, and church—and intercede for them. Maybe someday in heaven we will find that God answered our prayers and blessed our lives through the leaders we sometimes bemoaned.

## SUNDAY: Strap on the Belt of Truth

*Lord, today I want to bring these city leaders before you in prayer, for as King of kings and Lord of lords, you know all about leadership:*

Date: _____ Names: _____
(Use the following spaces for future weeks when you cycle again through these prayers.)

Date: _____ Names: _____

Date: _____ Names: _____

Date: _____ Names: _____

### Scriptures

*Lord, your Word teaches…*

> Stand firm then, with the belt of truth buckled around your waist (Ephesians 6:14).

> I urge, then, first of all, that petitions, prayers, intercession and thanksgiving be made for all people—for kings and all those in authority, that we may live peaceful and quiet lives in all godliness and holiness (1 Timothy 2:1-2).

### Daily Prayer Openers (for ourselves or others; see pages 72-73)

### Armor Prayer

Lord,

> I ask this Sunday that you "strap the belt of truth" on those in leadership, especially leaders in churches, schools, businesses, and government.

> I pray for (names of city and community leaders), that you put on them the "belt of truth."

> In a world filled with demonic lies and deception, where everyone lies to his neighbor and flatters with deception, it seems as

if leaders are especially tempted to lie, and in the midst of their deception they refuse to honor you.

O Lord, shine the light of your truth into their hearts and minds, and give us all the light of the knowledge of your glory displayed in the face of Jesus Christ. Amen.

> Ephesians 6:14; 2 Corinthians 4:4; Psalm 12:2; 1 Samuel 20:2; Jeremiah 9:6; Psalm 97:11; Psalm 63:11; 2 Corinthians 4:6.

## MONDAY: Make Fast the Breastplate of Righteousness

*Lord, today I bring these state leaders before your throne in prayer, for as King of kings and Lord of lords, you know all about leadership:*

Date: _____ Names: _____

Date: _____ Names: _____

Date: _____ Names: _____

Date: _____ Names: _____

## Scriptures

*Lord, your Word teaches...*

> Stand firm then...with the breastplate of righteousness in place (Ephesians 6:14).

> Restore us again, God our Savior,
>     and put away your displeasure toward us...
> [So that] love and faithfulness meet together;
>     righteousness and peace kiss each other.
> (Psalm 85:4,10)

Daily Prayer Openers (for ourselves or others; see pages 72-73)

Armor Prayer

Lord,

> I pray on this Monday that you "make fast the breastplate of righteousness," especially for leaders in churches, schools, businesses, and government.

> I pray for (names of state and county leaders), that you put on them the "breastplate of righteousness."

> In a world filled with demonic filth and impurity, give _____ the wisdom to live by your standards, for your Word says "Woe to him who builds his house by unrighteousness."

> Let them hear your voice and not harden their hearts, and if they do not yet know your love that you revealed in Jesus, please lead them to that all-important discovery.

> I pray that justice may roll down, in our state, like mighty waters, so that righteousness and peace may kiss together.

> I pray this in the name of the King of Righteousness. Amen.

> Ephesians 6:14; Ezekiel 23:42; Jeremiah 22:13 NKJV; Hebrews 3:15; Romans 8:39; Amos 5:24; Psalm 85:10; Isaiah 32:1.

## TUESDAY: Tread in the Shoes of Peace

*Lord, today I bring these national leaders before your throne in prayer, for as King of kings and Lord of lords, you know all about leadership:*

Date: _____ Names: _____

Date: _____ Names: _____

Date: _____ Names: _____

Date: _____ Names: _____

## Scriptures

*Lord, your Word teaches…*

> Stand firm then…with your feet fitted with the readiness that comes from the gospel of peace (Ephesians 6:14-15).

> The government will be on his shoulders. And he will be called…Prince of Peace (Isaiah 9:6).

## Daily Prayer Openers (for ourselves or others; see pages 72-73)

## Armor Prayer

Lord,

I pray on this Tuesday that you guide leaders to "tread in the shoes of peace," especially for leaders in churches, schools, businesses, and government.

I pray for (national and government leaders), that you help them become peacemakers and conflict-resolvers.

Leaders exercise incredible power in our world today; they have the ability to stir up or calm down, to foment division or bring healing and restoration, to wage war (even with nuclear weapons) or make peace.

Lord, cause them to pay attention to your commands, so we will have peace like a river and well-being like the waves of the sea.

You officials, be wise; you leaders, be warned. Amen.

> Ephesians 6:15; Acts 6:12; Psalm 140:2; Proverbs 29:8; Isaiah 48:18; Psalm 2:10.

## WEDNESDAY: Wield the Shield of Faith

*Lord, today I bring these business leaders before your throne in prayer, for as King of kings and Lord of lords, you know all about leadership:*

Date: _____ Names: _____

Date: _____ Names: _____

Date: _____ Names: _____

Date: _____ Names: _____

## Scriptures

*Lord, your Word teaches...*

> Stand firm then...[and] take up the shield of faith, with which you can extinguish all the flaming arrows of the evil one (Ephesians 6:14,16).

> We have different gifts, according to the grace given to each of us...if [your gift] is to lead, do it diligently (Romans 12:6,8).

## Daily Prayer Openers (for ourselves or others; see pages 72-73)

## Armor Prayer

Lord,

I pray on this Wednesday that you help leaders "wield the shield of faith," especially leaders in churches, schools, businesses, and government.

Please give (business leaders from your community), the wisdom they need to be leaders with great faith.

Your Word tells us that faith is the assurance of what we hope for, and the certainty of things unseen, but our world today is very unfriendly to faith.

In our culture today, people of faith are despised and mocked, and any reference to you is considered against the law.

Help our leaders to realize that the wealth of this world is like the grass that will wither and vanish away, but your Word, O Lord, is eternal.

Raise up leaders of Christian faith, O God, to lead in this leader-less world, and give them the humility that leadership requires. Amen.

> Matthew 8:10; Hebrews 11:1; Isaiah 40:6-8; 1 Peter 1:24-25; 1 Peter 5:5.

## THURSDAY: Think Within the Helmet of Salvation

*Lord, today I bring these leaders before your throne in prayer, for as King of kings and Lord of lords, you know all about leadership:*

Date: _____ Names: _____

Date: _____ Names: _____

Date: _____ Names: _____

Date: _____ Names: _____

## Scriptures

*Lord, your Word teaches…*

> Stand firm then… Take the helmet of salvation (Ephesians 6:14,17).

> How shall we escape if we ignore so great a salvation? (Hebrews 2:3).

## Daily Prayer Openers (for ourselves or others; see pages 72-73)

## Armor Prayer

Lord,

> On this Thursday please help leaders to "think within the helmet of salvation," especially leaders in churches, schools, businesses, and government.

> I pray for (academic leaders), that you put on them the helmet of salvation.

> Help them grasp that organizations are no stronger than their leaders; if leaders don't stand firm in faith, they won't stand at all.

> Help them see that the things of this world are like grass, which will be scorched, withered, and blown away.

> Open their minds to hunger for everlasting things, and to thirst for the joy of your eternal salvation.

> Protect us from leaders who think they know more than you, O God; how blind and foolish they are to think they know better than you.

> Above all, help them grasp that earthly knowledge and safety are of little value in comparison to never-ending salvation, which is found only through Jesus Christ. Amen.

> > Ephesians 6:17; Isaiah 7:9; 1 Peter 1:24; Psalm 1:4; Ecclesiastes 3:11; Psalm 51:12; Matthew 15:14; 1 Thessalonians 5:2; Isaiah 51:6; Acts 4:12.

## FRIDAY: Fight with the Sword of the Spirit

*Lord, today I bring these mission leaders before your throne in prayer, for as King of kings and Lord of lords, you know all about leadership:*

Date: _____ Names: _____

Date: _____ Names: _____

Date: _____ Names: _____

Date: _____ Names: _____

## Scriptures

*Lord, your Word teaches…*

> Stand firm then…Take the sword of the Spirit, which is the word of God (Ephesians 6:14,17).

> Oh, how I love your law!
>   I meditate on it all day long.
>                         (Psalm 119:97)

## Daily Prayer Openers (for ourselves or others; see pages 72-73)

## Armor Prayer

Lord,

On this Friday please help leaders to "fight with the sword of the Spirit," especially leaders in churches, schools, businesses, and government.

I pray for (missionary and parachurch leaders), that you would give them a hunger and thirst for your Word, and a desire to meditate on your Word day and night.

Help them to realize that the Word is their only offensive weapon, to be used by saying, as Jesus did, "It is written…"

May these leaders base their important decisions on your Word, O God, as revealed in the Bible.

May you spread the love of Jesus through the lives of these missionaries, and through the witness of their lives and words, I pray that many people, from all tongues, tribes, and nations, may be saved.

In the name of Jesus, the Word himself. Amen.

> Psalm 119:103; Psalm 1:2; Matthew 4:4, 7, 10; Psalm 119:46;
> Revelation 5:9-10; John 1:1.

## SATURDAY: Steadfastly Pray in the Spirit

*Lord, today I bring these church leaders before your throne in prayer, for as King of kings and Lord of lords, you know all about leadership:*

Date: _____ Names: _____

Date: _____ Names: _____

Date: _____ Names: _____

Date: _____ Names: _____

## Scriptures

*Lord, your Word teaches…*

Stand firm then…And pray in the Spirit on all occasions with all kinds of prayers and requests. With this in mind, be alert and always keep on praying for all the Lord's people (Ephesians 6:14,18).

Is anyone among you sick? Let them call the elders of the church to pray over them and anoint them with oil in the name of the Lord. And the prayer offered in faith will make the sick person well; the Lord will raise them up. If they have sinned, they will be forgiven (James 5:14-15).

Daily Prayer Openers (for ourselves or others; see pages 72-73)

Armor Prayer

Lord,

> On this Saturday, please help leaders to "steadfastly pray in the Spirit," especially leaders in churches, schools, businesses, and government.
>
> I pray for (leaders from your church), that you equip them and train them to be leaders in prayer.
>
> Teach them that the most important thing they can do each day is to pray, to draw close to you and seek to do your will.
>
> Give them the humility that leadership requires, for no human being knows the future.
>
> Give them the wisdom to gather people together for times of prayer, for when two or more are gathered, there you are in their midst.
>
> As your house is to be called a house of prayer, so may your leaders be humble servants, unified in prayer. Amen.
>
> > Matthew 6:33; James 4:6; Ecclesiastes 8:7; Ezra 8:21; Matthew 18:20; Luke 19:46.

Congratulations, you have completed one cycle of praying the armor of God!

When you finish this week's prayers, start over again on week one and pray the ten-week sequence again. Or, each week you may desire to pray the topic that is closest to your heart, such as marriages, children, or prodigals. Most of all, keep praying throughout the day for God to put his armor on you and those you love. Shalom!

# Small Group Leader's Guide

**P**raying the Armor of God can be used in a small group format to help Christians learn how to pray. We Christians often talk about prayer, but we actually tend to pray less than we talk about it. A small group setting is a terrific place, especially for new believers, to remedy this and learn to pray. Prayer, after all, involves language, and the learning and use of language is a social event.

I recommend a length of eight weeks for this small group study. After the first week, during which books are distributed, each group member is to read a small section before each meeting and to pray the daily prayer selections. During the group meetings, members again will read the daily prayers aloud, learning how to pray for themselves and then eventually how to adjust the names and pronouns as needed to pray for others.

In this way, people will experience personally how to pray the armor of God daily for those they love, and they also will learn how to modify the prayers from hearing others do so.

Godspeed!

# WEEK ONE
## Prayer Openers: Preparing Our Hearts to Pray the Armor of God

## Scripture

> Finally, be strong in the Lord and in his mighty power. Put on the full armor of God so that you can take your stand against the devil's schemes. For our struggle is not against flesh and blood, but against the rulers, against the authorities, against the powers of this dark world and against the spiritual forces of evil in the heavenly realms. Therefore put on the full armor of God, so that when the day of evil comes, you may be able to stand your ground, and after you have done everything, to stand (Ephesians 6:10-13).

## Study Questions

1. *Show and Tell:* Ask each person to take out his or her keys and explain what one key protects. Give a silly award to the person with the most keys, such as a fake "Key to the Group" (like the "Key to a City" that mayors often give visiting dignitaries) or a unique keychain. (The leaders can provide the gift or gag gift themselves each week, or they can assign a group member to bring the next week's gift, along the lines of an inexpensive candy bar or even a "white elephant" gift.)

2. Open with a prayer that God would help group members learn how to pray the armor of God in order to protect those they love, through the keys given in the Bible in Ephesians 6.

3. Read aloud and in unison Ephesians 6:10-13 (above).

4. Ask each person to agree to read one small section from *Praying the Armor of God* a week in preparation for the small group meeting and to pray the daily prayer each day. (Leaders may want to pre-purchase copies of the book to distribute at the meeting.)

5. Turn to the Contents page of the book and explain how the first letters of the days of the week correspond to each portion of the armor of God. Ask: What other memory devices do you use to remember important details (such as notes on the mirror, or string on a finger à la Uncle Billy in *It's a Wonderful Life*)?

6. Turn to pages 16-17 and read in unison Ephesians 6:13-18. What are your first impressions when you hear this passage? Does the idea of armor appeal to you or repel you? Why?

7. Even if the concept of war or fighting is repellent to you, what are some evidences that a spiritual battle is being waged about us?

8. How did your parents protect you when you were growing up? Were they overprotective or too lax? Who are you responsible to protect at this point in your life? Do you think parents or friends can improve at protecting their family or friends spiritually?

9. Discuss whether Christians can put the armor on themselves or whether it is better to ask God to put his armor on us (see pages 17-18).

10. Turn to page 71 and read the "Daily Prayer Openers" section aloud. Ask each person to consecutively read the prayers (pages 72-73), first for themselves and then for a person they would like to pray for. Assure people that no one will be forced to do this, but they will be encouraged to give it a try each week.

## Homework for Next Week

Ask each member to bring to the next group meeting a belt, especially one that is different or unique, and the group will vote for the most unique belt. Also, remind each person to pray the daily prayers for Week One (pages 75-86) and to read pages 25-29 before the next meeting.

# WEEK TWO
## SUNDAY: Strap on the Belt of Truth

## Scripture

Stand firm, then, with the belt of truth buckled around your waist (Ephesians 6:14).

## Study Questions

1. *Show and Tell*: Ask group members to show the belts they brought, and why they consider them to be unique. Vote for the most unique belt. Give a gag gift as a prize.

2. Open with a prayer that God would help each member of the group learn how to pray the armor of God through the keys given in Ephesians 6.

3. Read in unison Ephesians 6:10-13 (page 202) and 6:14 (above).

4. Have each person turn to Part Two, "Daily Prayer Openers," in *Praying the Armor of God*. Begin by praying in unison the first prayer on page 72. Ask the members to talk about their experience with praying the daily prayers each day last week.

5. Dress one group member up in a "tunic" by taking an old sheet, tearing it into the appropriate length and width, and cutting a slit for the head. Take a piece of rope and tie it about the person's waist, discussing how this is what the Bible referred to as "girding one's loins."

6. Ask if any group members sew and make their own clothing, or had a parent or grandparent that did so. Discuss how tailored, off-the-shelf clothing is a modern invention, and how our clothing would be different if we lived in the time of Jesus.

7. Ask: Does it surprise you that Americans lie so routinely, as Rick claims on page 27? Why or why not?

8. First-time Bible readers are sometimes surprised to learn that so many Bible characters tell lies. Does this surprise you or not? If the Bible were really a bunch of made-up stories and legends, would the heroes really be presented as so nonheroic?

9. What are some examples of little white lies we sometimes tell each other in order to not hurt the feelings of others? Examples may include: "It's nice to see you too," or "No, that dress doesn't make you look fat."

10. How about you? Does speaking the truth come easy for you, even when you know it will upset others? Or do you have a hard time in this area and find yourself saying little fibs or falsehoods?

11. Turn to Part Two, "Week One: Starting to Pray the Armor of God," and read the instructions aloud (page 75). Ask each person to consecutively read a prayer aloud (these are the prayers from last week).

## Homework for Next Week

Ask group members to wear vests to the group meeting. Let them know there will be a prize for the funniest vest. Encourage members to make their own or find a funny vest at a thrift store. (Feel free to tell the story about Rick's son Jesse, who, for a "Crazy Christmas Sweater Contest" at his church youth group, attached a wreath with five candles to the front of a sweater vest. He actually lit the candles, and for a time was a walking Advent wreath!)

Ask members to bring to next week's meeting a couple of old magazines they don't mind throwing away. Also, remind each person to pray the daily prayers for Week Two (pages 87-100) and to read pages 31-35 before the next meeting.

# WEEK THREE
## MONDAY: Make Fast the Breastplate of Righteousness

### Scripture

> Stand firm…with the breastplate of righteousness in place (Ephesians 6:14).

### Study Questions

1. *Show and Tell*: Vote for the funniest vest. Give a small gag gift (such as a candy bar) as a prize.

2. Open with a prayer that God would help group members learn how to better protect those they love by praying the armor of God.

3. Read in unison Ephesians 6:10-13 (page 202) and 6:14 (above).

4. Divide into teams of three or four people. From several old magazines available (use your own and the ones brought by group members), ask each person to tear out five examples of unrighteousness (keep them G-rated), as well as five examples of righteousness. Ask each team to explain their choices.

5. Ask: Why did you pick some magazine pages as examples of righteousness and others of unrighteousness? How would you define righteousness? Unrighteousness?

6. Do you agree that we live in a world that misunderstands or devalues righteousness? Why or why not?

7. Have you ever known someone who assumed he or she would go to heaven after death simply by being "a pretty good person"? Why do you think people make that assumption, especially about such an important matter (where they will live for all eternity)?

8. Mention an event or decision in your life in which you followed your heart and did something that seemed wise at

the time, but later you realized was a very poor and foolish choice. Examples might include a purchase, an investment, a romance, a decision involving your family, friends, or church. How do you think it was possible for your heart to lead you so astray?

9. Why do you think the Bible describes righteousness as a "heart issue," as Rick mentioned on page 32? What is it about the heart that makes it the place humans choose between right and wrong?

10. Have different group members read from Psalm 119:11, Proverbs 3:1-4, Proverbs 3:5-6, Ephesians 5:18-20, and Luke 6:43-45. What do these verses suggest about how we are to manage our hearts?

11. Turn to Part Two, "Week Two: Learning to Pray for our Families," and read the instructions aloud (page 87). Ask each person to consecutively read a prayer aloud (these are the prayers from last week).

## Homework for Next Week

It's "Crazy Shoe Contest," so ask members to wear their craziest shoes to the group meeting. Let them know there will be a prize for the most original shoes. Encourage members to be inventive or even outlandish. Encourage them to pray the daily prayers for Week Three (pages 101-111) and to read pages 37-41 before the next meeting.

## WEEK FOUR
### TUESDAY: Tread in the Shoes of Peace

## Scripture

> Stand firm…with your feet fitted with the readiness that comes from the gospel of peace (Ephesians 6:14-15).

## Study Questions

1. *Show and Tell*: It's time for the "Crazy Shoe Contest." Vote for the most creative pair of shoes. Give a small gag gift as a prize.

2. Open with a prayer that God would help group members learn how to better protect those they love by praying the armor of God, through the keys given in Ephesians 6.

3. Read in unison Ephesians 6:10-13 (page 202) and 6:14-15 (above).

4. Ask: Have you ever had a job or played in a sport that required a special type of shoe? What was it? Were the shoes of use anywhere else? Did the shoes require any special preparation? Discuss how this relates to our need to prepare for conflict in advance by being clothed with an attitude of peace.

5. Ask: Describe a close friendship you once had that fell apart. What were the factors that led to the failure of the friendship? In hindsight, is there anything you would do differently to try to avoid what happened?

6. Discuss the fact that the Greek word translated "demon" in the New Testament is derived from a word that means "divider," and that Satan himself might therefore be called the Great Divider. What are some areas in which demonic divisiveness is manifested?

7. Have group members read aloud John 14:27, John 16:33, Philippians 4:6-7, Romans 13:14, Galatians 2:20, and

Colossians 3:15. How do these verses suggest we can become persons of peace?

8. Is it always possible to keep the peace? Read and discuss Romans 12:18.

9. Turn to Part Two, "Week Three: Praying to Be Clothed with Christ," and read the instructions aloud (page 101). Ask each person to consecutively read a prayer aloud (these are the prayers from last week).

## Homework for Next Week

Ask each member to bring something that works as a shield in today's world. For instance, sunglasses shield our eyes from harmful light. Announce there will be a prize for the shield that most corresponds to the spiritual message Paul was trying to convey by the Roman shield. Encourage everyone to pray the daily prayers for Week Four (pages 113-124) and to read pages 43-48 before the next meeting.

# WEEK FIVE
## WEDNESDAY: Wield the Shield of Faith

## Scripture

In addition to all this, take up the shield of faith, with which you can extinguish all the flaming arrows of the evil one (Ephesians 6:16).

## Study Questions

1. *Show and Tell*: Ask group members to explain the shields they brought and how they correspond with the spiritual shield of Ephesians 6:16. Vote for the best shield and give a small gag gift as a prize.

2. Open with a prayer that God would help everyone learn how to pray the armor of God.

3. Read in unison Ephesians 6:10-13 (page 202) and 6:16 (above).

4. Ask: What is your favorite day of the week? Least favorite? Why do you think Wednesdays have been so disliked over the centuries?

5. Some people talk as if faith is opposed to reason. Did you ever feel that people of faith were uneducated or misled? Why or why not?

6. Ask members to read aloud from Hebrews 11:1, Genesis 15:6, Romans 4:1-3, Habakkuk 2:4, and Romans 1:17. Can your group summarize, in contemporary words, the main point of these passages?

7. Have different group members read aloud from Proverbs 1:7; 3:5-8; 26:12; Isaiah 5:21-24; and Psalm 23:1-3. Do you struggle with living by faith in God, which means trusting God and following his ways, rather than living by faith in yourself? Why or why not?

8. The shield specified by Paul in Ephesians 6:16 is the larger Roman shield, rather than the smaller shield used in hand-to-hand combat. Why did Paul choose one rather than the other?

9. Rick says on page 45, "Here's the point: the shield of faith was never meant to be used by solo Christians. The shield of faith is to be used in formation, alongside other Christians who have also taken up their shield, their *thureos* of faith." Based on this, how do you believe God designed Christians to function: alone or with others, and to what extent? Why is this sometimes difficult?

10. Read aloud Romans 12:1-8 and 1 Corinthians 12:12-31. If the Bible says we are like members of the body, how deeply involved does that imply Christians should be in their churches?

11. Turn to Part Two, "Week Four: Praying for Spouses and Marriages," and read the instructions aloud (page 113). Ask each person to consecutively read a prayer aloud (these are the prayers from last week).

## Homework for Next Week

It's the perennial favorite, "Crazy Hat Contest," so ask members to bring their favorite hat, cap, or helmet, along with whatever hat they think might win the award for best hat. Encourage everyone to pray the daily prayers for Week Five (pages 125-137) and to read pages 49-52 before the next meeting.

## WEEK SIX
### THURSDAY: Think Within the Helmet of Salvation

## Scripture

Take the helmet of salvation (Ephesians 6:17).

## Study Questions

1. *Show and Tell*: It's time for the "Crazy Hat Contest." Vote for the best hat and give a small gag gift as the prize.

2. Open with a prayer that God would help members of the group learn how to better protect those they love by praying the armor of God.

3. Read in unison Ephesians 6:10-13 (page 202) and 6:17 (above).

4. Ask: What are some slogans that you remember from TV commercials, such as Wendy's "Where's the beef?" Alka-Seltzer's "I can't believe I ate the whole thing," and Super Bowl champions saying, "I'm going to Disneyland"? Nominate and then vote for the group's choice of the all-time best advertising slogan.

5. Do you agree that there is a battle going on today for the minds of people? Do you think this battle is happening in the natural or in the spiritual realm? Who is winning?

6. Read Philippians 4:6-7. Are there any group members who are worrywarts? Have each person describe one issue in life that they tend to worry about.

7. Read 2 Corinthians 10:3-5. How can Christians "take captive every thought to make it obedient to Christ"? How can we win the war on the battlefield in our brain?

8. Turn to Part Two, "Week Five: Praying for Friends and Single Adults," and read the instructions aloud (page 125). Ask each

person to consecutively read a prayer aloud (these are the prayers from last week).

## Homework for Next Week

Ask group members to bring the oldest Bible they own, as well as their favorite Bible verse to share (and to be ready to explain why it is meaningful). Encourage everyone to pray the daily prayers for Week Six (pages 139-151) and to read pages 53-57 before the next meeting.

## WEEK SEVEN
### FRIDAY: Fight with the Sword of the Spirit

## Scripture

> Take...the sword of the Spirit, which is the word of God (Ephesians 6:17).

## Study Questions

1. *Show and Tell*: It's "Sword of the Spirit" week, so ask the members to show the old Bibles they brought and to share their favorite Bible verse. Also, ask each person to explain why the verse is meaningful. Give a small gift to the person with the oldest Bible.

2. Open with a prayer that God would help each member of the group learn how to better pray the armor of God.

3. Read in unison Ephesians 6:10-13 (page 202) and 6:17 (above).

4. Have different group members read aloud a consecutive verse each from Matthew 4:1-11. Ask: What strikes you most about this encounter? Do you think the devil did this only to Jesus, or does he tempt all humans, albeit more subtly? If Satan were to ask you these questions, how do you (without knowing what Jesus did) think you would have responded? Would you or the devil have won this skirmish?

5. Have the parents in the room reflect on their experience of teaching their children how to talk. How does this relate to our need as Christians to learn to speak with God? How does God's Word help us learn to communicate with God?

6. Ask: How many people remember the days of computers that used DOS? Was it easy or difficult to install programs? How is Scripture, in Rick's terminology, "self-installing"?

7. Discuss various methods of reading and saturating oneself

with Scripture so that it can self-install in our minds, hearts, and even souls.

8. Turn to Part Two, "Week Six: Praying for Children and Teenagers," and read the instructions aloud (pages 139-140). Ask each person to consecutively read a prayer aloud (these are the prayers from last week).

## Homework for Next Week

"My Favorite Prayer" contest. Ask group members to bring a copy of their favorite prayers and be ready to describe why they are meaningful. Examples may include the Serenity Prayer, the Twenty-Third Psalm, the Lord's Prayer, or the Prayer of Saint Francis. (Suggest they bring several copies to share, if possible.) Encourage everyone to pray the daily prayers for Week Seven (pages 153-164) and to read pages 59-64 before the next meeting.

# WEEK EIGHT
## SATURDAY: Steadfastly Pray in the Spirit

## Scripture

> And pray in the Spirit on all occasions with all kinds of prayers and requests. With this in mind, be alert and always keep on praying for all the Lord's people (Ephesians 6:18).

## Study Questions

1. *Show and Tell*: Ask group members to read aloud the favorite prayers they brought and to describe why they are so meaningful. Rather than voting for the best prayer, the group leaders might choose to give a final gift to each member, such as a bookmark with the Lord's Prayer, on this final meeting of this group study.

2. Open with a prayer, thanking God for teaching the group how to protect those they love by praying the armor of God, and for drawing the members closer together in fellowship.

3. Read in unison Ephesians 6:10-13 (page 202) and 6:18 (above).

4. Ask: Are you a workaholic? Why or why not? Would your spouse agree with your answer? Your boss or coworkers? Your pastor?

5. Ask: Are you good at taking vacations? Why or why not? What is the best vacation you have ever taken? What was the most restful?

6. Discuss the historical fact that Yahweh, the God of Israel, is the only deity who commanded his followers to *rest*. Brainstorm the reasons Yahweh might have had for this unique command.

7. When is your Sabbath? When do you take a break, kick up your feet, and rest?

8. Some Christians sleep in on Sundays because it is their "only day to rest." Do you think this is a valid reason for missing church? Why or why not?

9. Ask: Do you consider yourself good at praying? Why or why not? How is prayer a form of resting in God?

10. Have different group members read aloud from Psalm 25:1-3; 32:10; 56:3-4; and Ephesians 5:18-20.

11. Discuss the assurance we Christians have that, no matter how difficult or sorrowful this world may be, we will enjoy perfect and eternal rest on the new earth. Ask each member to discuss one burden they look forward to being relieved of in our eternal state.

12. Turn to Part Two, "Week Seven: Praying for Men," and read the instructions aloud (pages 153-154). Ask each person to consecutively read a prayer aloud (these are the prayers from last week). Since this is the last group meeting, explain there are still three weeks of directed prayers for the group members to complete on their own (or you may choose as a group to continue meeting for those three weeks). When the ten weekly prayer guides are completed, encourage everyone to start again and continue cycling through the guided prayers for as long as they desire.

13. Close in prayer, asking each person to pray a prayer of spiritual protection for the other members of the group, using whatever item of armor they desire to pray for the group as a whole. In this manner, the group will end by a unified effort to protect one another by praying on the armor of God.

# Notes

1.  Dietrich Bonhoeffer, *The Cost of Discipleship* (New York: Macmillan, 1949, 1963), 201.

2.  Wilbur Fields, *The Glorious Church* (Joplin, MO: College Press, 1960), 189.

3.  Mark D. Roberts, *Dare to Be True* (Colorado Springs, CO: WaterBrook Press, 2003), 4.

4.  Daniel Goleman, *Working with Emotional Intelligence* (New York: Bantam Books, 1998), 16-17.

5.  Fields, *Glorious Church*, 191.

6.  William Perkins, *Works* (1603), 906. Perkins also was the author of the Latin phrase, *fidei vita vera vita*, which means "The true life is the life of faith." If a person were to memorize only one Latin phrase, this would be a good candidate.

7.  G.K. Chesterton, *The Autobiography of G.K. Chesterton* (San Francisco: St. Ignatius Press, 2006), 217.

8.  Fields, *Glorious Church*, 191.

9.  Henry H. Halley, *Halley's Bible Handbook* (Grand Rapids, MI: Zondervan, 1927, 1965), 18.

10. Ibid., 19.

11. Ronald Reagan, "Address to the National Religious Broadcasters Convention," Sheraton Washington Hotel, Washington, DC, January 30, 1984.

12. George Gallup Jr. and Jim Castelli, *The People's Religion: American Faith in the 90s* (New York: Macmillan, 1989), 60.

13. *Active* was derived from the Greek root *energes,* from which evolved our English word *energy. Energes* can be translated "effective," "active," or "powerful." Bauer, Arndt, Gingrich, *A Greek/ English Lexicon of the New Testament and Other Early Christian Literature* (Chicago: University of Chicago Press, 1957), 265. In addition, from the time of Aristotle, *energes* meant "active." Gerhard Kittel and Gerhard Friedrich, *Theological Dictionary of the New Testament*, trans. and ed. Geoffrey W. Bromiley (Grand Rapids, MI. William B. Eerdmans Publishing Company, 1964), vol. 2, 652.

14. William L. Lane noted in his commentary on Hebrews, "The description of God's Word as...'living and effective,' signifies that it is a performative; it possesses the power to effect its own result." William L. Lane, *Hebrews 1-8, Word Biblical Commentary,* Volume 47a (Dallas, TX: Word Books, 1991), 103.

15. Daniel Boorstin, *The Discoverers* (New York: Vintage Books, 1983), 14.

16. "So long as man marked his life only by the cycles of nature—the changing seasons, the waxing or waning moon—he remained a prisoner of nature." Ibid., 12.

17. Ibid., 13.

18. Thomas Cahill, *The Gift of the Jews* (New York: Doubleday, 1998), 144. Cahill also waxes eloquently in his discussion of the Sabbath on how the innovation of a day of rest paved the way for education and even the notion of the universal right to education.

# Acknowledgments and Thanks

*"I thank my God every time I remember you."*
*(Philippians 1:3)*

- My wife, Amy, the love of my life and my greatest encourager.
- Our three children, Micah, Noah, and Jesse, to whom this book is dedicated.
- Don and Gay Stedman, my parents and lifelong models of love and integrity.
- My in-laws Dean and Marcia Holst, siblings Randy and Teri, and the rest of our extended family. Thanks for the joys of family that God pours on us through you.
- Our church, Adventure Christian Church of Roseville, California. You are the best! I truly love you and love being your pastor.
- My administrative assistant, Lori Clark. Thanks for your help—with everything!
- Our church staff. Thanks to each of you for so capably leading your ministries, thus freeing me to do mine.
- Our church elders. Thanks for your unfailing love, faithfulness, and encouragement.
- Thanks to Janet Grant, my agent, and to Terry Glaspey, Rod Morris, and the rest of the team at Harvest House. Working with you on this project has been a true pleasure, and I look forward to our collaboration on the next two books in this series.
- Last but certainly not least, my church reading team: Bev Graham, Bryan Hardwick, Carol Peterson, Jennifer Edwards, Lori Clark, Nick Domich, and Vivian Jones; and my prayer team: Art and Truda Pauly, Rick and Janet Perez, Chuck and Janine Robson, Michael and Pam Tijerina, and Bill and June Twelker. Thank you for the expertise and effort you put into this project. I treasure each of you.

# About the Author

Dr. Rick Stedman is a collector of classic rock-and-roll vinyl LPs, bookaholic, author, philosopher, pastor, and devoted husband and father. For two decades he founded and led Adventure Christian Church in Roseville, California, a church that in ten years grew from zero to five thousand in spite of the fact that Rick listens to his records as he writes his sermons.

Rick has graduate degrees in theology, philosophy, and ministry, and has been a guest on various radio shows, including *Focus on the Family*. For relaxation he likes to read, mow the lawn with his tractor, tinker in his workshop, and watch movies with his wife and best friend, Amy.

Further resources for praying the armor of God, including sermon outlines, illustrations, and other pastoral resources, are available at prayingthearmorofgod.com. Rick can be reached at rick@rickstedman.com, and his blog is also available at rickstedman.com